Albert Bright

AF175363

AstronTimeOnomy Solutions

Volume 1 of:

GlobalOnomy

Astronomy-Rules to Optimize:

Economy & Currency, Knowledge & Wisdom, Freedom & Liberty, Health & Wealth, Welfare & Sustainability - World-Wide.

This book arose from the fascination of the universe with its seemingly limitless dimensions and growth - and the idea of using its laws of nature as a recipe for a better world.

Albert Bright

© 2015 Albert Bright
   1. German edition: 2016

© 2021 Albert Bright
   1. British edition: 2021

Printed by:
BoD, Books on Demand GmbH, Norderstedt, Germany

ISBN: Paperback: 978-3-7526-0286-9

9 783752 602869

Publisher: www.world-wide-wealth.com

Authors: Albert Bright

Envelope design, illustration: Albert Bright, editor,
proofreading: www.world-wide-wealth.com

Translation: www.world-wide-wealth.com

Printed in Germany

Bibliographic information of the German National Library:

The German National Library records this publication in the German National Bibliography; detailed bibliographic data can be found on the Internet via http://dnb.d-nb.de Available.

Table

I. INTRODUCTION

Time. For most people, time is just what the watch shows. But time has enormous dimensions. Time itself is relative. And time relativizes.

This book relativizes many dimensions of our lives. Relativizes - not destroys. Property is preserved. And many other current constellations will also benefit from the changes. But concerning the new dimensions, much of actual constellations meanings and influences are relativized. And much more freedom will lead to a huge increase in wealth. Many obstacles are removed. "Just" by giving each individual access to their property: the "power" or "dimension" of his own life "time". And through a "bonus" everyone gets the freedom to use this time for their own purposes and priorities. Without artificial barriers hindering them to make their way. There are a lot of barriers, which we do not question, as we grow up with them. Rules from family, friends, neighbors, capital, society, education, work, religion, sport, Maslow-"Needs" Just take some time, to relax. And think about what life you are living. Yours - or others one?

i. DIMENSION & VALUE IDEAS ABOUT TIME

B.1. General aspects of the Time

For most people, time is just what the watch shows. But time is an enormous, powerful physical-astronomical power and dimension. Planets optimize their orbits in close correlation to time aspects. Space-time aspects, such as Albert Einstein discovered.

Let us look "deeper" than just at the time on our watch. Then we will discover that time also determines and optimizes our "orbits" around our "stars". And we must optimize our time and orbits around our own chosen stars and galaxies. Without enough own energy and/or speed for our own way, it will be a star letting us "crash" on it. Then we will be "optimized" in its sense. We will have to arrange ourselves with its rules and its space-time.

In the "developed" worlds we are extremely driven by time. Our time is determined by clocks, alarms, meals, work, meetings, goals, projects, appointments, media, sports, news, sleep time... . From kindergarten, school, study, work, up to retirement, much is determined "externally". Most of us are "pushed", hour by hour, day after day. The weekend is just a small break. At the end of the month there is a small salary joy. But "life" is postponed into the holidays for a few weeks.

Take what you get. And not: get what you really want yourself, is valid for many of us.

Planets are also "born" in a galaxy. But planets continuously optimize their orbits, their paths. People should be able to do that as well. Specially, because they have an additional capacity: they can think. Why then, so little people change their orbits? We think, that this due to less "liberty" in comparison to the planets in Universe. As well it is due to low "energy", and to too little "time"(-awareness)! We will have a look at these aspects. We will focus on time as a power and dimension. We will determine what "influence" it has. And we will show that it is able to influence the other dimensions, in its individual way.

Time has time. It is an enormous force. Nobody and nothing have more time than time. It's time for the time. Time, for a new time epoch.

B.2. Historical aspects of the Time.

No regime has survived for a long time. Hence: no regime knows what "the best way" is. Therefore, the markets should be allowed to go where they want to go. No interventions to divert. At least not, unless human rights are injured.

"Time heals all wounds". But the wounds are smaller when no "powerful" politicians try to get things into their direction.

B.3. Life aspects of the Time

In our world, time has established itself as an aspect that accompanies us in all areas of life. Time is like an additional type of exchange medium.

At the top of a coexistence, people live by "air and love". Time seems to be endless at the beginning of a relationship. Time "investment" in a private relationship "pays off". Not in money-aspects, but certainly in humanity values.

On the precipice of coexistence, there lie hatred and death. Time will end its influence in the case of death.

While with love, time seems endless, at death it gets the value of zero.

Somewhere between these two extremes lies the economic sector. The primary exchange medium here today is "money". But here, as well, time is an elementary qualitative factor in the field of economic relation management. And time is a central aspect for all measurements, such as: profitability, work-time recordings, balance sheet aspects, ...

Thus, after all these general thoughts about the time we will now focus on the astronomical significance of time. And as well on its correlations and influence on business and economy, on society and sociology.

In the book "Astron-Economy Solutions" (Albert Bright, British Library, 2014) we analyzed many parallel aspects of astronomy and economy - and developed:

1) an economic formula approach based on Albert Einstein´s Simple Relativity formula

and

2) an approach on the importance of "circles"/ orbits in astronomy - and its significance and transferability to the economy.

After these fundamental thoughts in this actual (and those of the last) book, we now want to focus, on the next "obvious" correlation between astronomy and economy ...

O The 4th dimension in universe is "time"
O The 4th dimension in the economy is "money" - at least for the moment ...

B.4. Universal aspects of the time

Time is the oldest dimension of our university. The universe is existing since 13,800,000,000 years; our solar system for 4,600,000,000 years; the earth started 40.000.000 years after the solar system launch; humanity exists since 200,000 years; the Christian time since 2021 years; Democracy, the Industrial Revolution and the first economic model are barely 300 years old; the Special Theory of Relativity 116 years - and the General Theory of Relativity of Albert Einstein 106 years young. Time is of central importance. It is time to reconsider its value and "contribution" to astronomy and economy aspects.

B.5. Relativity aspects of the time

At the extremes of existing formulas there is no more time "visible". If everything changes into energy (Albert Einstein) or gravity (Newton extrapolated, according to Albert Bright), then time is only "hidden". It is on the other side of the respective equation(-s- correlation). It is in a "stand by"-position, waiting for a change of conditions.

But even in our "real" life dimension, "time" is a relative dimension.

"Time" accompanies objects, creatures and ideas. And depending on the surrounding correlations, the "lifetime" of objects, creatures or ideas can be of zero to (almost) endless.

Before the big-bang, the surrounding forces were so strong, that nothing in that location was able to develop. No time counting "for something" (as in our "real life") could begin. With the big-bang, the first of the 13.8 billion years, that universe exists, could start to count.

Before the French Revolution, the surrounding forces were so strong that no liberty was able to develop. With Gutenberg's invention of modern printing in 1450, knowledge, theoretically, could spread and establish itself quickly – but it was blocked for long time. In 1616 Galileo Galilei was still condemned by the Catholic Church (which, incidentally, it only revised in 1992) and his knowledge was banished. Despite Gutenberg´s books-printing and know how spreading possibilities. It was not until 1799 that the French Revolution marked the beginning of the first year of a new "general" existence in "liberty". That big-bang is just 200 years ago ...

The time of each "star", each (person's) life, each government, every company, each idea still differs enormously, depending on the circumstances surrounding it.

There are "rules" of coexistence in universe. And on earth as well. And there seem to be correlations between the two areas*³.

In the universe, each planet can go/optimize its own way - and does it, as Einstein discovered. For 13.8 billion years the universe has been growing. And it is continuously growing faster, as Hubble discovered. The "universe" provides the stars and planets with "space-liberty" (or "space-richness"). If it could not grow, it would collapse, as research revealed. Without growth, today's economies will also collapse.

The new freedom achieved on earth in 1799 led to enormous growth in knowledge, economy and general prosperity. Unfortunately, the pace of growth has slowed down due to various – primarily – political "forces". These "forces" include the implementation of an enormous bureaucracy apparatus and more and more statal interventions. These "forces" reduce liberty. They are slowing down the potentially higher growth and wealth.

A first correlation between astronomical liberty, "space wealth", and (potential) "world wealth" (with more liberty and longer life on earth) can be shown with one example of the relativity of time:

A "paradox" addressed i.a. by Stephen Hawking: The "time" on two absolutely identical clocks runs faster at the top of a hill. And slower at the bottom of the hill.

This paradox gets (seemingly) bigger, when considering, that the most aged people live in higher locations.

The "life" (lifetime) passes by, slower at the top - and faster at the bottom of the hill. This (from our point of view) is due to more "power" resulting from more "centrifugal force" at the top of the hill. The more "energy/power" – the longer the lifetime of any material thing or creature.

In our opinion, this is no paradox. It has to do with time-relativity. The "time-power" at the top of a hill is confronted with more centrifugal-force-power. And it is more remote from the gravitational-center-power. Gravitation does not slow down – and centrifugal force gives liberty. Time, as such, runs faster. Together with all other aspects at the top of that hill. And when running faster, there is more energy involved. This reduces the "power" of time (see formula of time, later). And by reducing the "killing forces" of time, life of persons and matter can be longer. The opposite is valid at the bottom of the hill. This is due to more of the life-destroying force of gravity and more power of time (see formula, later).*5

The farer away from a gravitational-power-point, the stronger gets the power of (life-pushing) "space-power". And the weaker gets is the power of (life-destroying) "time-power". *6

Saying this, the paradox addressed i.a. by Stephen Hawking is no more a paradox at all, anymore. ☺ .

Gravity appears as "disturbing" force. It is a type of "central(-ization) force", which does not allow other matter-parts to go their own way in the universe. Too much gravity destroys very much. This can be seen in super-nova implosions and black holes. And also in central-plan-economic systems. And as well in systems claiming only one centrally dictated "truth" to be followed. Without contradiction. Like communism or religions in the past.

We can live longer at the top of the hills (symbolically set equal to freedom) because our "energy" is not "braked" by too much gravity- nor time-power. With more freedom for our own path, we can live longer - and generate more prosperity.

Gravity also works in our society. The more a state (or other power) restricts liberty, the more we become bound to these systems. The less freedom we will have to develop ourselves (further).

If the star's gravity grows too much and too much space-power is suppressed, then the planets slide to "bottom" - towards the "space-hole" (lack of space-power) at the (central) star. This is valid especially, if planets do not have enough own energy or/and speed (=energy) to continue their own path with their own space-force. (By this we will later disprove and straighten Einstein´s "curved space" towards "space-power-concentration"-levels.*6).

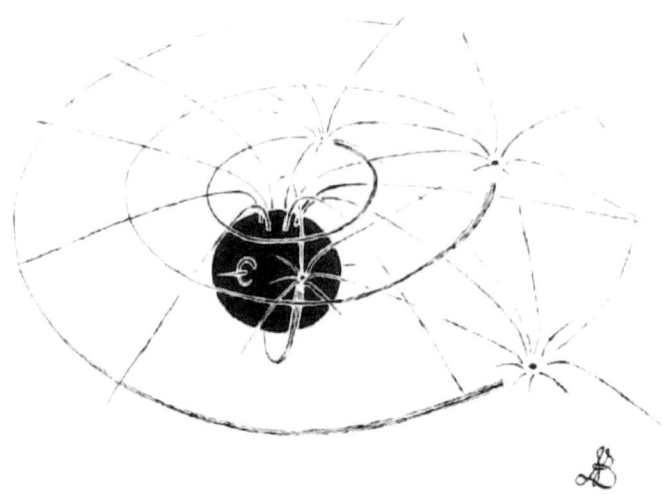

And if the star as such becomes too big, its own gravity will even destroy himself. Stars destroy themselves by means of a super nova:

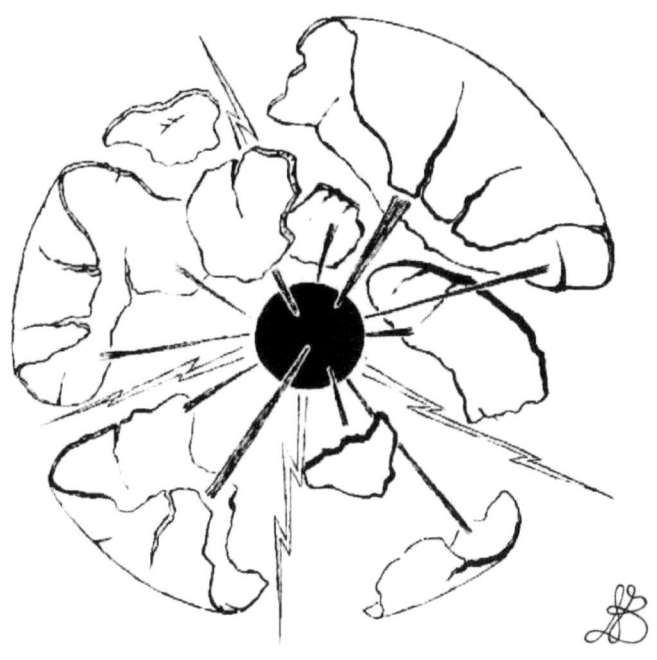

It's like a suicide. "Too big to survive" - and not "too big to fail" - is valid, if we look at it with astronomical rules. "Too big to survive" has been shown to us so much times in history that we seemingly are not able to see "the forest due to too many trees". (A list of some historical developments will be presented later.)

The "too big" urgently need to be downsized.

Otherwise, they will implode - and their implosion will lead to dramatic loss of wealth. After a super nova, at the end of the "(supernovae) time", nothing remains. Just dust.

And this "too big" not only applies to territorial invasions, or states "confiscating" anything. It also applies to other aspects – such as the aspect of too much money:

A) Too much money (in former times ...): If there is too much cash flow in an economy – this leads to a rise in prices. And too much inflation will end up in a devaluation - similar to a super-nova-implosion ...

B) Too much money (in today's times ...): If the money is only "produced" to compensate 1) government and bank debt due to errors in speculation, or 2) to try to reduce the currency value, to increase one's own competitiveness or 3) just to try to save the "too big to fail" – this will not lead to inflation in prices. But will "only" lead to a bloating of the "virtual" money. This will happen without reference to the real values of the "normal" "real world". And the explosion of this "virtual money bubble" also leads to a devaluation of (among other things) government papers. This is similar to a super-nova effect. At least, if (!) there is no relativization of this bloating. We will show later.

Time has shown it - and time will show it again.

Focusing on gravity/centralization is not good. Neither for stars nor for governments. Nor for planets, nor companies.

Since Keynes's state-demand-policy-theory, many aspects of centralization - and debt in incredible dimensions – have been "established". Too much debt deprives the market from cash flow - and drains the rest of the "universe." This can lead to an implosion: economic crisis, a devaluation or a currency reform.

The "power" of the "planets" (businesses and citizens) is reduced. And in the worst case everything is destroyed. That is:

O The more freedom/space, the less time-destructing forces, the more "real-time"/space to survive.

O The more freedom, the more wealth can be generated.

O The less centralization, the less damage from individual errors.

O Speed ("X" space, matter or energy - in "Y" time units) is a key to improving a lot. It is a key to the

freedom of one's own space paths. And to keep distance: far from star gravity and black holes. Far from (freedom) space absorption centers.
Nobody is perfect. This also applies to states and governments. We urgently need to reduce centralization - and increase freedom again. In all areas of life. For individuals, companies and countries.

Planets optimize their own way - within a solar community. There is a "give and take"- balanced by the star, according to Newton

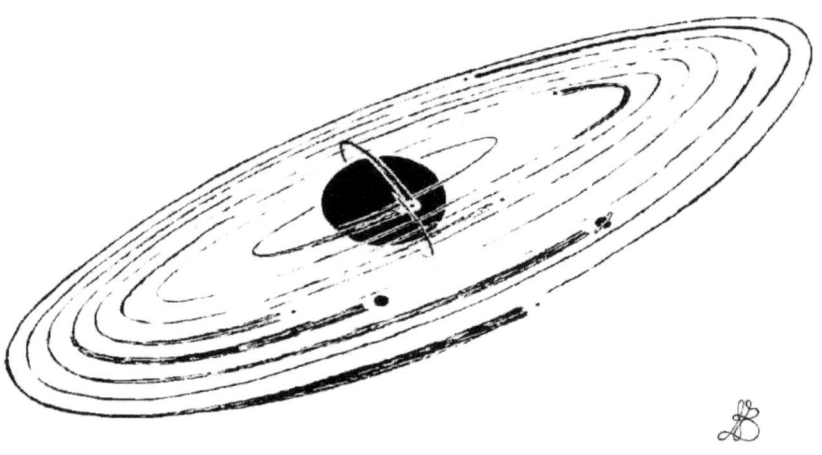

or balanced by the space-absorption and curved space, according to Einstein

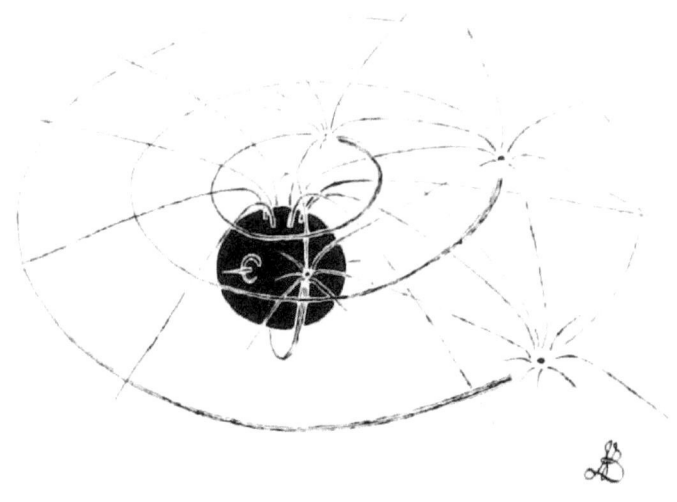

((Please keep in mind, that we will later disprove this theory of Albert Einstein. It is not about space-absorption, but about space concentration and space-power-generating to be able to go own ways. This freedom generates expansion, (free) space (wealth) in the Universe)).

Time is relative - and patient. And there still seems to be time to respond. But if nothing happens, the rules of the universe will bring all back. Back to "nothing": astronomy-rules will lead to the implosion of all these current virtual bubbles. Time will tell.

B.6. Physical aspects of the Time

A.) Base Dimensions

Time is within the physical base dimensions:

	Base	Characters
a. Length relative dimension	Meters	m
b. Mass specific Dimension	Kilograms	kg
c. Time extensive Dimension	Second	S
d. Electrical Electricity intense Dimension	Amps	A
e. Temperature process dimension	Kelvin	K
f. Quantity of fabric energetic dimension	Mol	Mol
g. Luminous intensity field dimension	Candela	cd

B.) Room dimensions

Time is the fourth dimension for space. Einstein's curved space-time dimension has revolutionized astronomical theories. It shows that time (in its sense of a period) is a central aspect for the curvy course of the planetary orbits around their respective star. (Curvy, not straight; straight only appears(!) to be shorter - as more direct. But at a round star, the curved way in direction of a pole is shorter than the straight way going "horizontal".).

Time is also an aspect for the "own search" of the planets for the most possible "liberty" within the its orbit around the star:

1st : curved, not straight: Search for the shortest way around the star, when being close to the star on the orbit part, (see above).

2nd: elliptical(!) orbit i.e.: with the shortest possible dwell and route of its orbit being close-to(!) the star, in order to float freely (!) in the universe for as long as possible - and

C.) Direction

Time is the only dimension that goes only in one "direction" - no return is possible (according to current consideration and knowledge).

D.) Simple Relativity Aspect

$$E = m * c^2$$

Time wasn´t an aspect of Albert Einstein's Special Relativity Theory formula. At least not until we added some add-ons. See later…

E.) Adaptability and continuity

Time is that dimension in universe, which qualifies best to be checked for correlations and formulas to possibly optimize money-aspects on earth.

Time itself is difficult to influence. Two aspects with which "individual time" can be influenced are 1.) about speed - and 2.) turning away from gravity. But the "general time" will continue in its direction. Time – as opposite to money - can't arbitrarily be changed or exchanged. No falsification is possible. Time is always correlated to matter-aspects. And "inflation" is less possible than with money: you can't just print more time.

There is a third "power" capable of indirectly influencing time. It is 3.) a big bang: Time, in our opinion, (re-)arises in the universe with every birth of a new star (for example resulting from a concentration of neutron nebulae). So, with higher birth rates (each birth is a kind of big-bang) the amount or power of time can be extended as such. With each birth, of mankind on earth, there is also a value correlated – a human being – and not "nothing", as in the current printing of money. And 4.) the fourth power that can affect time is the death of living beings, or the end (a super-nova) of stars. No time is valid for them anymore.

All these aspects will be considered in our new economy- and finance-model.

F.) Visibility of time

It has always been a challenge and wish, to make time visible. However, all these instruments only show our interpretation of time. Time itself is invisible:

a) Water clocks
The oldest clocks of the "western" side of the world are estimated to have been created in 1600 B.C. They were found in Egypt and Babylon. However, some authors claim that these watches were already released in China in 4000 B.C. These water clocks were certainly invented by astronomers. This is because with the water-system, time as well could be measured at night, while observing the stars.

b) Sundials

   b.1. Tekhenu ("obelisc" in Greek) are the oldest (3500 B.C.) monuments designed by Egyptian astronomers to measure time. They are high buildings made of stone, like a nail, four-sided, with a pyramid-like shape at the top. The time was measured by the shadow on the ground - but no real "system" for accurate time measurement was found.

b.2. Shadow watches: the oldest of them: 1500 B.C. Also found in Egypt. It had a tekhenu rod on a flat stone with markings like "hours" at the shadow-side on it. Now the "time" could be determined a little bit more precisely. This technology lasted until the 17th century, with various optimizations.

c) Hourglas

   Sand "flows" through a small hole from one glass flask to another. Time now could also be recorded on ships (water systems did not work on ships - due to movements). The earliest guess of when they were invented is 150 B.C., in Alexandria.

d) Mechanical watches

The first invention of a mechanical watch was realized in China in 1100 B.C.. It was operated by a feed-trigger-mechanism.

e) Clocks

They were invented in 1602 by Galileo Galilei. It stayed as the leading technology up to the 1930s.

f) Electronic watches

The first electronic clock was invented in 1840. But electricity still was not far spread. So success began 100 years later, in the 1930s .

g) Quartz watches

They were invented in the United States in 1927. They were not widely distributed until the 1980s, when production costs fell.

h) Atomic clocks

Atomic clocks were invented in the United States in 1949. The most accurate was built in Switzerland in 2004. It has an inaccuracy of 1 second in 30,000,000 years.

All these attempts to make time visible show how important and fascinating time has always been for humanity.

G.) Frequency / amount of time

There are many different views about time. Allow us to add another one ...

Time seems endless. But in our opinion, time exists only because matter, space and energy are present.

And if energy is relative and limited, then time also must be relative and limited.

After the Big Bang, a limited amount of energy has emerged - and a limited amount of time, in close correlation and dependence on the other forces.

For a certain amount of energy/ matter/ space – there is a corresponding amount of time. The more concentrated the matter, the greater the amount of "concentrated" time, which this matter "carries". The half-life-time of Th-isotop232 is 14,050,000,000 years. People may live 120 years. Flies 1 Day.

When the first "carrier" of time "dies", time is "handed over" to a "successor" – which can also be something else (1st: sun, 2nd: super nova in-/explosion-energy, 3rd: quasar, 4th: dust, 5th: new star via big-bang from neutron-dust-concentration). Time is able to adapt to different circumstances, depending on the environment.

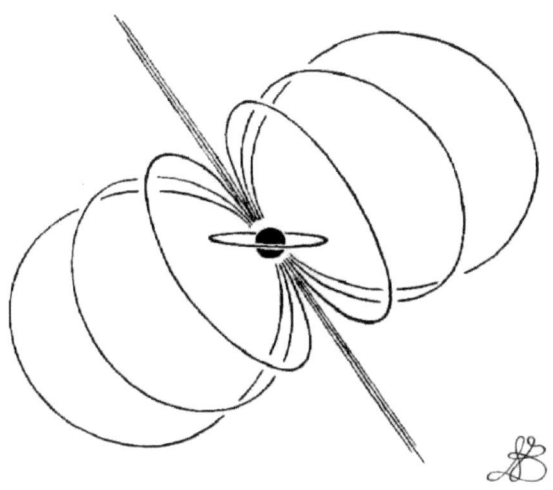

The "life time" of any matter - or human - can be increased by "investing" energy (also indirectly):

Nuclear material can be enriched. People can consume better meals through investment of effort and research. And doing so, live longer. Lifetime as well can increase with investments in better medicine. But this time and energy that you gain had to be invested / consumed / taken away from somewhere else. In total, for time – as such – there is a maximum. It is sim-

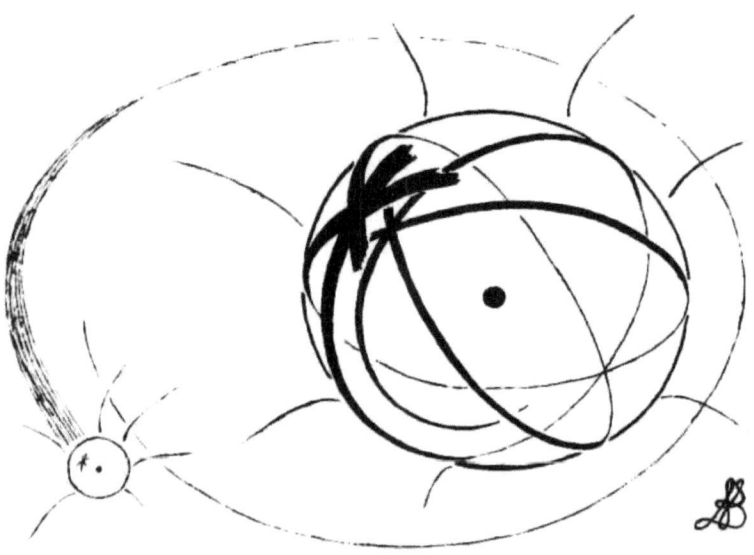

ilar to the amount of maximal energy.

H.) The formula of time

Time, in our opinion, surrounds its object / its carrier(!) like a strong(!) bubble. Time is carrier-immanent! And as strong, as its carrier.

The time-quantity (time bubble) is not (primarily) a correlation of the three space-dimensions and the fourth space-time dimension in a kind of "soap bubble". The time-bubble dimension primarily results as a direct correlation of a certain matter/ energy combination.

This can - in our opinion*** - be shown by re-thinking: by changing a little bit Einstein's formula:

((*** Paradigm-shift: Please be aware, that the following mathematical equation could have been solved by children in school. But we had endless discussions with astronomy-professors, which insisted, that you can´t use Albert Einstein´s "c" to be separated towards time and space. "c" is a constant factor, that was calculated by lots of tests and extrapolations. It is the light speed-constant, a maximum of speed, unique, not changeable. We did anyway – without being able to verify our thoughts at the time of publishing the first book in 2014. We could verify 3 years later (2017) in the book AstronRaumOnomie. But the point is, that even today a lot of scientists behave like the church in former times: "The earth is flat – and the center of universe. That's it!" I was lucky in 2 aspects. 1) I could not be excommunicated as Galileo Galilei, as I am not in any church at all. 2) Due to that prohibitions about the "c", I was the lucky one, that invented the time-formula. And a tremendous breakthough. A paradigm-shift, into new discoveries within astronomy. And a new "picture" of our universe.))

$E = M * C^2$ ("M" = matter, in capital-letter, to distinguish from the "m" = meter used for the new formula)

$E = M*(300,000*1,000 \text{ m/s})^2$

> By this, "km" changes to "m" (as basic unit).
>
> $300,000 * 1000\text{m} =!= \text{"d"}$
>
> "d" =!= constant: "time distance"

$E = M*(d/s)^2$

> Extracting a root from this, we get:

$\sqrt{E} = \sqrt{M} * (d/s)$

> Dividing by $\sqrt{M}$, leads to

$\sqrt{E} / \sqrt{M} = d/s$

> Solving this equation for s, leads to the <u>Time formula</u>

$$s = d * (\sqrt{M} / \sqrt{E})$$

Or simplified

time = matter / energy
T = M / E

"s" defined as "time" means:

If all matter converts into energy the above formula would give a zero at M and would be divided by endless E . The result is a zero. This multiplied by d would be zero. That means, time would disappear when matter disappears. Time is carrier-immanent!

By the way, the same (time disappearing) happens, if matter would fly at (close to?) square light speed (our interpretation of Einstein´s formula). In this scenario the constant "one-directional-time-way-line" would also disappear. There would be something infinite. Something without the force of

time, (close to?) destroying its carrier. And therefore, there will be no ageing as such any more.
("Close to", as square-light-velocity might not be
achievable, as more energy might be needed, as
that possible energy resulting from the equation.
And: Energy is limited.).

This "disappearance" of time at (approximately)
square light speed does not mean that this "M" will
die, since for this particle no "Time" prevails any
more. In our physic view the opposite is valid here.
Time just has (almost) no more influence (!)
(strives towards zero). And since time has (almost) no influence anymore, the "life" for this mat-
ter-particle can be endless. Already (almost) completely transformed into energy, this is "only" an
alternative relativity-state of matter.
Mathematically: (M: close to) zero divided by (E:
close to) endless leads to "close to zero", (means
"something" remains).

And vice versa, if matter becomes "stronger"
(larger, for example if two planets or stars collide)
but "energy" is lost (due to the being cold(er) of
one of the planets, or by loss of speed due to the
impact), then "M" increases, and "E" decreases.
And if M increases, then according to the above
formula the time "s" for this matter/ energy constellation increases. But here, the reverse is true:

there is not more, but less life time! Time has more "power" in this constellation – and influences the lifetime of the M-particle in a negative way. As M grew, gravity is also larger now. The greater the gravity, the more likely it is to create a super-nova or a black hole. Both destroys everything like matter (without any speed). All is converted into dust and/or energy. At black holes even this dust and energy and/ or light might be absorbed.

Mathematically: (M: close to) endless divided by (E: close to) zero leads to "nothing" (as: "something" divided by "zero", mathematically is not defined. This means "nothing" remains).

(Behind these last two constellations another "secret"/ discovery is hidden. I added it as a mosaic in the 3rd book/volume: the correlations between time and space).

This formula however must be right. It is as well shown in the (former) "paradox" of the two identical clocks. The time at the summit of a mountain runs faster than the time at sea level. This is due to more centrifugal speed (energy increasing) and less gravity. Faster going time means: less influence of the time-dimension (less matter-influence / more energy-influence). Time is not braking things (clocks) any more with its gravitational part of matter in its formula. This increases the life-time at the summit; and decreases life-time at the sea level). Greater centrifugal-speed (is nothing else than a kind of energy) relativizes (reduced) the power of time (according to the above formula).

The (life) time dimension of an object/subject differs in dependency of matter/energy/speed constellations. Therefore, the lifetime of the Th isotope is longer than that of a human being. And a small company with a lot of "energy" will live longer than low-energy state-owned enterprises. At least in normal competitive markets. Without government interventions.

The time dimension will always be as big as "d" multiplied with the respective matter/energy amount AND correlation. Therefor one can imagine time as a smaller "picture" (with low matter/energy numbers) or a larger "picture" (with greater numbers). Thus, time surrounds matter/energy object like a balloon, less or more inflated, depending on: a) The magnitude of the figures of matter and energy as such. And b) as well depending on the correlation between matter and energy ((means: 1) more (or increasing) matter (more) than energy leads to a growing time-power; 2) more (or increasing) energy (more) than matter leads to decreasing power of time)) .

In former times astronomers thought, that (life-) time (of matter) will never end. This is derived from the realization that matter, with extreme acceleration, becomes hot and thus expands. This expansion becomes extreme before reaching the square light speed. However, the energy required to achieve the square speed of light is greater than the energy, E, which should result from this velocity-increase out of the matter. Since energy is limited, this will not happen!

But with our formula, matter may convert completely into energy. This happens in reality at for example a super-nova. There might remain a quasar, or develop a black-hole. But it is possible, that nothing at all remains. No matter means zero at the numerator of the fraction – and a big number at the denominator of the fraction. Zero divided by whatever number remains zero. If there is no matter anymore, no time-counting is needed anymore, as time is (matter or) "carrier" oriented. The dimension of time disappears – at least for the matter of that super-nova. There are other dimensions, which loves to take over – or replace – the former power of time 😉 .

In our book "Astronomic Solutions" (British Library, 2014) we relativized Einstein´s Special-Relativity via extrapolation of Newton towards an extreme gravitation, that can destroy everything (Extrapolated gravity is Energy) . This is not the current trend in the universe. But this tendency (gravity = centralization-power) can be observed again and again on Earth. What a pity. This is one of the reasons, we address the economic challenges showing astronomy-solutions by publishing this book.

One of the dimensions that will take over the energy resulting from a super-nova is the dimension of space(-growth). And: one of the biggest forces in universe is expansion. Thus, instead of striving for gravity and time, we should focus on "space" and "liberty" in order to do as good as universe. ((Our book AstronSpaceOnomy (AstronRaumOnomie, Deutsche Nationalbibliothek, 2019) will focus on this)).

C. Time aspects in the GlobalOnomy Model
TIME - AND ITS INTERDEPENDENCIES

Time is an astronomical dimension. Stephen Hawking writes in his book "A Briefer History of Time" in the last sentence of the first chapter: "Time (whatever that may be), will show." - Not: "when", but: "what"-ever "that" may be. Time is (was) a mysterious and highly regarded dimension. As well for physicists and astronomers.

Time seems to have been born in the big bang (at least in our current dimension-thoughts). Together with the other dimensions (space, matter, energy ...). Time is one of the most mysterious dimensions. It can´t be touched like matter, can´t be visited like a chamber (space, room). And it "only runs into one direction".
((This direction aspect applies at least to every existence (things or living beings). In our extrapolations, time may change into 2 directions: In the case of (close by) |E| (via c²), time is meaningless and existence-time is endless. At (close by) |G| time is enormous and existence-time equals zero)).

After a super-nova (i.e. death, the end of the time of a star that has grown too big or/and a star with too little energy or speed) a new star can emerge. It may emerge from the dust-clouds that resulted in the in- & explosion of the super-nova. A new beginning of time for a new star after the death of an old star. (For closer inspection see: "Astronomic Solutions", Albert Bright, 2014).

One could expect a "cycle" of time because it seems to die and resurrect again, albeit in other objects or subjects. As well existence-time is limited - and relative.

Similar aspects apply as well on our world. Such as at the ups and downs of nations: the Egyptians, Greeks, Spaniards, Portuguese, French, Dutch, Danes, Germans, Americans ... If a regime becomes too big (and suffers additionally from diminishing "energy"/ "power") it will implode – over time ... And something new will emerge from the "remaining dust" of the old system - when the time is ripe.

In the Astron-Economy model, we used the formula of Albert Einstein's Special-Relativity-Theory as a basis. Here we transfer the physical dimensions into economic dimensions:

$E = m * c^2$ has been transformed to $W = M * V^2$, where: W = wealth; M = matter (represents the product and service market – and all involved aspects, like machines and humans); and V^2 = velocity, stands for speed or efficiency of production.

First, the transferability (of the forces and dimensions) towards economy, was analyzed. Then the circuits/orbits in the model were examined for their functionality, since models only work, if there is a continuous (growing) circulation (a repetition of cause and result).

Time was the last dimension analyzed in this circular analysis within the Astron-Economy-Model-book - but "last" did not mean "most meaningless". I wanted to pay special attention to "time" - within this actual book.

a)   The role of time in "W", Wealth

Time is of great importance for wealth. And since time is a long-term dimension, far-sighted concepts are the most successful. At least in the long term. And the long term is urgently needed for more sustainability.

A farsighted vision is always stronger than short-sighted actionism. The individual steps towards vision must be vision-oriented.

Until about 530 years ago (1492), before America was discovered, many people believed in the world being flat. And being the center of the universe. That is not long ago - compared to the

200,000 years of "modern" human history.

And in these 530 years many great empires were built – and destroyed. Again and again ...

... and out of the largest companies listed 100 years ago, only less than 1% still exist.

Whereas the universe grows over time, humanity seems to be working against time. Or against many rules that apply in combination with the time dimension. This destroys wealth, including potential ones.

Wealth is generated according to the formula $W = M * V^2$ with matter and time aspects (speed, productivity).

If there is something in correlation within the formula, that becomes too large in comparison to the other dimensions, an imbalance arises. This, at a certain limit, cannot be compensated. The system will collapse.

Too much (virtual) "wealth" (bubbles), "W", on the left side of the equation without the "aspects" of the right side being able to follow, will lead to a collapse of a (bubble-) "system". Or at least of a part of it (e.g. that of the currency, evaluating the "wealth").

And regarding "M": Too big or less-productive M will lead to a decreasing speed/ productivity "V":

1) too much investment in unproductive or less-productive state sectors (such as: a) weapons and soldiers for "imperial" expansions or b) election-winning, via not financeable promises) or

2) too many government interventions (such as: too much bailout money to focus on only adminis-trative or speculative sectors such as banks - and neglecting the maintenance of real-economy pro-ductive sectors.

If M increases, V must decrease, to cope with equation requirements. And since this "V" has a "V^2" potentiated meaning, the negative effect on wealth is greater than the positive aspects of ac-tionist "investments" or "interventions" against the rules. Real productive sectors will suffer. Wealth will be destroyed.

Time has shown - and time continues to show.

b) The Role of the Time at "=": Rules and Legislation

We need rules to generate wealth. This is the central aspect of the character "=", as equation rule. Without rules or with unequal rules such as

">" or "<", no general and multiplicative wealth can arise. At least not the best possible "wealth of humanity". Only as the "wealth of some". And the "only wealth for some" has repeatedly led to revolutions and/ or crises. After such crises, often greater prosperity for all was achieved. Over time. But it would have happened much sooner and with much less wealth destruction, if the right rules would have been applied earlier.

"Some" can never consume as much as "humanity". So "revolutions," which empower more people to achieve wealth, always lead to a general increase in wealth. As well for the capital itself, which today is mainly maintained by the "some".

This does not mean that a redistribution of current wealth by politics should take place through state intervention. This has been tried in the past in the so-called "social market economy" – and failed miserably. Wealth is more concentrated today than ever before.

The next "revolution" must, in my opinion, be against many rules and forces established by "all-prescribing politicians". It must be a revolution towards more freedom of the individual. This "revolution" must go into the direction of less state rules and fewer interventions.

The "=" character is only a symbol which leads us to the dimensions that really are important in order to increase prosperity: "M" and "V²". The "=" itself (rules and laws of state), does not produce anything. If …
a) there are too much regulations;
b) the "=" weighs too heavily via strong penalties;
c) the "=" has too much influence on the right and/ or left of the equation;
d) regulating interventions, are to strong,
… then the level of wealth (left side of the wealth equation) will decrease. This is because the freedom of action of the productive forces (right of the equation) is restricted. Too much "energy" must be spent on formalistic and non-productive regulating state-aspects.

If jurisdiction itself is a/ the main "value" for the state (as an institution - acting for profiling or power) – and focused against the freedom of individuals, this will end in poverty. If jurisdiction (over-regulation of things) even "advances" to be a profitable sector for investment (when being able to earn millions even with stupid accusations), then the "wealth"-creating forces are no longer on the right side of the equation. Power will be concentrated in the "middle", at the "=". This hinders the generating of true prosperity. It shifts "prosperity of humanity" towards "institutional prosperity", without any real wealth generating power.

In Einstein energy-formula of Simple-Relativity ($E = M * c^2$), the "=" character "itself" has no value. It only is a rule-symbol for his ideas on the right side of the equation: to determine the quantity of energy out of matter.

There are aspects, which humanity has developed out of the "=". E.g. the "Liberté, Egalité, Fraternité" of the French Revolution. These are aspects that can greatly increase well-being on the left side of the wealth equation. Nevertheless, the achievements of the French Revolution, among other things, lack of a central word: "Réalisabilité", feasibility. Only "equality" does not lead to prosperity. And too much influence of "politics and rules", the bureaucratism and centralism that arose after the revolution, hinder(d) growth (right side ...) and thus: wealth (left side ...) of the equation).

In the universe there is a tendency towards equilibrium. Automatically. Without any state intervening. The same rules apply to our Earth. State intervention did not lead to the targeted redistribution of wealth in the past. Quantitative easing has led to a tremendous increase in money supply. But this only lead to very marginal growth. Because about 80% of this money increase "landed" in hidden places. This money primarily remains at the un-productive bubbles. And, more in depth, a large part ends at "Bad-Banks-Sub-Accounts". All transactions hidden away from reality. The rest of the money ends up as speculative money: many (share-)prices rose to never seen dimensions, although not much had changed in real terms.

Billions of quantitative easing did not lead to "real" growth of the net social product - in almost no state. And the "too big to fail" are rather "to big to survive". The Money landed there for "stabilization" as "system-relevant" is lacking at small and medium-sized enterprises – which by the way employ more than 80% of the population. Capital was more important than people. The "real" growth of the past was created "despite" and not "because" of state intervention. Alternatives are needed.

The smaller the "=" …
    and thus
    a) the amount of rules and
    b) the time required to fulfill these rules – or
    c) the "power" needed in court to fight against

them,

… the more time for productivity, the more prosperity can be generated.

Time has shown it - and will continue to show it.

c) The role of time in "M", "Matter"

At the end we all are dead. But in meantime we can do a lot with our time.

The importance of time is immense for the cycles of the (partial) actors and their relationships within that "M", "matter", in our economy-definition. All are acting for growth and wealth as a) entrepreneurs, b) workers, c) consumers, d) government, etc. As well on a time-basis - as described in the book "Astron-Economy Solutions", Albert Bright, 2015). Since the Industrial Revolution, which began in the second half of the 18th century, time has been one of the most important success factors in mass production.

Time penetrated into all areas of life. For every type of business time importance grew steadily. Today, even milliseconds decide on profit or loss in the speculative area.

In this book, I don't want to write about all the

things we know about time in our normal working life. As well I will not focus on important aspects for entrepreneurs in terms of time. A main focus will be an area which I only mentioned marginally in the last book (Astron-Economy-Solutions): "Exchange media". This will be done in the next main(!) chapter ("D." Money Aspects in the GlobalOnomy-Model).

d) The role of time in "V²", Speed / Productivity

The importance of time in astronomy is so great that we kept Einstein´s squaring of his "c" ($E=m*c^2$) as well for our "V". We also potentiate the time-including Variable "V" in the Astron-Economic-Formula. Time is the central basis for all industries in all countries for all types of production up to all types of speculative models.

D. Money Aspects in the GlobalOnomy-Model

In earlier times, the exchange processes between different goods were quite difficult. Sometimes you had to exchange a lot of chicken eggs for rabbits first, and then you could exchange the rabbits for sheep's wool.

Exchange media have been developed to be able to exchange things more "directly" (faster, i.e. time has influenced these developments ...).

So, rabbits and eggs were replaced by gold, silver, steel coins, paper banknotes, virtual money .... And since no regime trusts the other, almost each state developed its own money. In 195 officially recognized states there are 160 officially recognized currencies. Additionally, there are particular developments of "independent currencies" at various companies, banks, etc. Diversity is growing. In 1945, there were 50 main countries - and the most important international currency was the dollar. Today we have 195 countries - and the dollar continuously gets new competition of new developments.

Trust. If each country or company creates its own money – which (exchange-) currency can we still trust?

In former times, money had a fixed value. Thus, each currency could be exchanged for a certain amount of gold - at fixed exchange rates: the so-called "gold standard". But the gold standard was abandoned due to political reasons. In the same way, the relationship between money-value versus the "real values" within a country (gross domestic product) was abandoned in favor of "rescue" actions and speculation.

What is the "real value" of the money? Let's analyze the "money" approach with astronomy aspects.

What role does "money" play in $E = m * c^2$ or $W = M * V^2$?

a) W (wealth) - according to E (Energy)

If you fry rabbits or eggs on a fire, you can eat them. If you fry gold at least its value remains, in order to buy something to eat. A roasted banknote isn't really tasteful nor nutritious – and loses its value when roasted. And roasted virtual money cannot even be touched, tasted nor eaten.

Speculation against the British Pound led to its

devaluation of 30% in 1992 – and to the "off" for England's accession to the € countries. However, the UK real economy has not shrunk by 30%. The British economy retained its value. Despite currency devaluation, there was no big crisis.

When Switzerland decoupled the SFR from the fixed correlation with the €, its currency-value rose by 20%, even though the Swiss central bank's debt rose to the highest level ever. So far, their economy has not really suffered from this step.

Almost all governments have increased their "money" amount by 10 times in the last 15 years (reference point is 2015). This means 1,000% since the "New Economy" bubble in 2000. Or even shorter: since the real estate and bad-bank bubbles of banks and state, dramatically growing since latest 2008. But they have not really boosted GDP (gross domestic product) growth. Only the stock increased - but "only" by 300% .... With great ups and downs all times. This means that:

1) up to 700% of the 1,000% "money -wonder":

a) landed in bad-banks (very well hidden by any government and/ or bank) or
b) was urgently needed for bank cash flow,

since no bank has lent any money not even to another bank because of mutual distrust

or

c) was only printed to devalue one's own currency, to promote the "own" industry. By facilitating exports and making imports more difficult. Because own-money value decreases and lower export-prices to higher value-currency-countries. And at the same time, this increases import prices.

2) By achieving only 0.5% growth p.a., even the first mentioned 300% were mainly used for speculation. That has nothing to do with "real" growth for more "general"(!) wealth

3) There has been a huge shift in wealth to the richest countries, companies and individuals - and the middle and lower sectors lost wealth;

4) 300% speculation did not lead to wealth growth – but mainly to re-distribution;

5) Due to the large debts (resulting from a.o. mis-speculations by the state and banks), all central banks, prescribed low interest rates. Otherwise states/banks would not have been able to serve their annuities.

6) Since no investor was willing to invest money for such low interest rates, the states offered high price discounts on their debt securities. This again causes problems in the long-term, when re-financing these loan amounts.

7) Since discounts and refinancing papers would not have been financially viable in the medium term, it was necessary to withdraw the sale of these securities from the open market. They were led towards central banks like ECB. They bought these papers in dimensions of: "whatever it takes" at very low interest rates: Down to zero!

8) The interest rate reduction led to difficulties at insurance companies. Now also they had to be "supported". The measures taken reduced additionally the assets of private persons at insurance-polices. In addition to the negative interest rates for all the savings-money on bank accounts.

9) There was very much money being destroyed by mis-speculation. And more money required for interventions and inter-

est payments on (hided) bad-bank projects. Thus, nothing of the 1,000% of fresh money landed in the real economy nor at most of private individuals. This led to big cash-flow-problems. Particularly in the politically less "powerful" middle-class.

10)   At least there was no inflation for goods and services (due to the acute cash flow shortage – and the money "needed" for other things …). Inflation would have destroyed even more in the private sector.

11)   But, due to no inflation, the state debt will not "automatically" be reduced, like in the past. This will lead to problems with re-financing in the near future.

12)   Total debt, re-financing and new/ additional debt have steadily increased since J.M. Keynes' demand policy in the 1970s. Governments and central banks, at some level, will no longer be credible. State bankruptcies and/or currency reforms will come. Or: better solutions (than the repetitions of the past) must be invented and implemented. With this book, we contribute to one potential alternative. One of these better solutions - which does not lead to a crisis and

impoverishment of the population. In our view, the one and only global one.

All the above sketched, signals again that 1) the economy can always handle reality aspects; 2) the monetary policy and interventions by the states do not really lead to the wealth of nations, but rather to the wealth of the 1% richest - and 3) that even the 1% richest have primarily "virtual" money, which cannot be touched, fried, nor eaten.

Our current "money" doesn't really contribute to wealth. It only accelerates and increases trans-actions within homemade bubbles.

To stop this vicious circle of endless money-gen-erating, a drastic relativization of the actual values is needed. See chapter "F".

Out of (virtual) money, no "real" energy/ wealth can be generated.

b) "=" (Rules)

Since the "W" (on the left side of equation ($W = M * V^2$) is over-rated with a currency bloating, the as-pects of the right side of the equation must be up-graded in the same way. De facto, however, M threatens to fall(!), due to crises. Moreover, a mere reassessment is not a real growth in wealth. They are just numbers, as we will show. And there is no such possibility of appreciation for "E" in our astronomical basis, means for our model (E => $W = M * V^2$).

There is nothing in the universe that represents our kind of "money."

There is not even just one currency for the whole world. Therefore, the problem of misleading (de-)valuations between the individual currencies comes on top. Realistic competition for the best products and services would increase the wealth of nations. Automatically. Far fairer. But political currency wars mislead wealth.

A high level of "W" upgraded via speculation-earnings of the 1% best performing "platforms" politically always should be kept at that level. And even growing. Then, in order to keep "=" (and not change by ">" or "<") the state must intervene. It must buy and keep shares at high prices – at least from the biggest "visible" companies: The "too big to fail" ones. And if it is not the state directly, it might as well be the countries central banks or even the ECB, as we have seen.

c) "m" or "M"

In the "M" sector, money has taken the role of the exchange medium. But it is continuously and increasingly being abused by politics, banks and the speculative sectors. The "power" of money is continuously being devaluated. Worth-figures in "money-values" do not really have that value at "realistic" terms and views. Specially because of the former mentioned over-valuations, which are needed to keep the "W" at a high level.

Nevertheless, whatever comes out of these misleading tendencies, the economy can manage any currency(-change). However it might be evaluated, as previously shown.

That is very good news. At least on the one side.

On the other side, negative effects on general wealth may get worse:
The economy always must try to achieve stable growth - no matter what happens around it.

Therefore, economy seems to "automatically" mimic what the universe suggests: autonomy - as far as possible. Going an independent, own path. Like the planets optimize their orbits around their stars (as to Albert Einstein). And if social-states regulate too much for employees, companies must make other aspects more flexible. For example: almost shorter contracts, virtually (false-)self-employed, self-employed, autonomous, automatization (machines instead of employees), production outside of the country, etc. All this, in order to keep a realistic value. This must withstand a devaluation of the "political"-value.

The central difference of universe is, that: in universe there are no misleading interventions of a state. Thus, universe is faster and far more stable than the economy. Economy is constantly resisting – and adapting to new interventions. In order to be able to keep on its orbit. Against all statal activities. That costs "energy" which otherwise could have been used for more productive aspects.

In universe there is 1) no state, that centralizes everything; 2) there is a huge – not controllable - amount of galaxies; 3) the galaxies are very widely distributed and therefore unaffectable; and 4) galaxies go their own way. Therefore, misleading trends or collisions will be very regionally limited, without much impact on the rest of the universe.

By contrast, interventions by (the relative "powerful" and relative few) states on our planet can destroy the prosperity and constellations of the normal "orbits" of humanity.

The contribution of money towards wealth in today's world is no longer a real contribution, as shown in "a)". Money nowadays has a rather disturbing or even destructive effect (due to the endless "production" of it, to "save" the economy). This is the reason why in the previous book (Astron-Economic Solutions) the section title of the exchange-media was "alternative exchange media". And "money" was only presented as the current (provisional) solution.

That is why we believe that our actual "money" should be replaced by something else. More on this will be presented later.

d) "c²" or "V²", Speed

The greater the demand, the faster the rate of circulation of money, the more credit is granted, the hotter the growth of the economy, the more money is needed and would have to be printed. And, to avoid inflation, the government must raise interest rates. That is the theory. The reality is different:

There is a lot of fresh money, although there is no increased demand in "real economic". The circulation speed of money is at a very low level – at least on the real-market. The economy has cooled down. The main "heat" (by the multiplicator "V²" is generated in the speculative sector. And since the states themselves are affected, they do not raise interest rates. This would harm themselves. Now, no longer only the 'others' are disadvantaged (by inflation): the economy and the private sector, as usual in the past.

The problem: more and more money is needed for losses and annuities of false speculations of the past. These mistakes are hidden in "bad-banks" and false values within speculation bubbles. Inflation does not take place in the markets of the real economy, but only on the speculative bubble side. As there was no inflation, there was no reason to increase interests rates. Without higher rates on statal papers, money goes to speculation – and can´t be stopped, as there are not better alternatives. Additionally, states would not have been able to continue to finance their own past mistakes, if interests would have risen. "Inflation" comes indirectly - through a devaluation of government securities, which is ultimately the same technical procedure – and pushes speculation. But the obvious, real problem is greater.

For a 100% "value" of a state paper the "market" will only be willing to pay less and less. Instead of

100%, more and more papers are being processed with a disagio provided – i.e. only 90%, 80%, 70% ... of its formal value on the paper are paid. This compensates for the risk of a possible devaluation of these statal "securities", which results, when states are no longer able to pay for all outstanding debts.

If only 70% are being payed for government "securities", 30% more debt "securities"-paper-value are to be issued. That is, 130% to replace(!) (pay back) a 100% (old) debt. Total debt continuously increases dramatically. New(!) required debt not taken into account. The speculative adding-on value via (mainly) increasing the multiplicator "V^2" with "politically" 130%, does not lead to real value of the real economy. Nor to real wealth.

A vicious circle that ends in a fiasco. At a certain point the "markets" are no longer prepared to risk investing in "securities". As well states on the medium term are no longer able to finance the high discounts. This is why the European Central Bank was "needed", to buy everything, "costing whatever it takes". After all, the ECB can "print" the required "money" even without collateral financing. And if no companies (not even the top firms (!)) no longer get any money from their banks, because "the eurozone banking system is over-sized, undercapitalized and de facto insolvent" ("WirtschaftsWoche" and "Welt" Newspapers/magazines, 07-2014), then the ECB "must" also meet (big) companies capital requirements. Politically they are "too big to fail" ... With additional "printed" money. Smaller companies, which employ 80% of mankind, are not being helped. Capital, in the actual system, counts more than people.

And this is hard to stop, since no centrally regulating "state" or "institution" can regulate this "inflation". Nor will it. Because all "instances" are directly involved in this catastrophe. And all "players" are able to produce money. In 160 different currency types and even more ways. And in endlessly different speculative models. One replacing the former. A self-made vicious circle in an unprecedented dimension. Worthless money and government securities are debt bubbles, that can hardly be repaid. And the papers of the speculative bubbles, from a certain moment onwards, will not be bought anymore. And their values will end in nothingness. If nothing important is done.

The main problem here is not government papers, as the states with their tax options are behind these papers. They may be able to repay the debt within a long period of time. The main problems arise from speculative models: where "real" money has to "fight" against 5,000% speculative capital - or worse. There is no real counter-value behind these bets. And states and institutions are often guaranteeing or even involved. And these bubbles do not arise successively, within 10 or 20 years, but within days or even seconds - without the possibility, in this short time, to change the rules of the game.

The problem is that speculative capital is 50 to 100 times greater than the "value" of the real economy.

And by being able to achieve much more "value" in a much shorter time, the banks and states jumped on these models in order to be able to repay their debts - or just to make money.

The real economy, when all money is being invested in speculation, will hardly get any money/cash flow at all. Real economy cannot promise nor generate similar large sums of theoretical turnover and profits as speculation bubbles suggests.

This results in an automatic mathematical "problem" with the formula derived from astronomy. The "real" matter will implode because (in our current capital/money-driven economy models) it no longer has the "energy" to "run" (no: "power to do work" - as "energy is described in astronomy).

And if too many of the sectors within the "M" become negative (or zero), our "matter-oriented" economy will "implode". A negative figure (or zero) multiplied with whatever "upgraded" "V^2" will lead to a negative (or worthless) "W".

The energy of our current economy will swash to other sectors. If this is productive in a common sense, it will be right. But if it only is speculative, one will win and one will lose. There will be no(!) real(!) additional(!) value(!). And if bubbles explode, no value remains at all.

When the pace of "real" growth of many sectors of the real-economy becomes negative, the effect of the overall "V^2" ("efficiency") will become smaller (with a negative tendency). At the latest by this time wealth "W" will be destroyed. And, as we can't live from bubbles, also a lot of speculative capital will end up in nothingness.

The "healthy" rate of monetary "disruption" (i.e. inflation) is "set" at 2% in the "real" economy in order to achieve a "stimulating" growth effect. Less could be recession lead. More could lead to undesirable inflation.

A "sick" rate of money destruction is called hyper-inflation. In the real sector its about 10%+. In the speculative area, it seems to be at approximately 100% when becoming dangerous. 100% per year resulted in about 1,000% additional money supply compared to the level of the early years of this millennium.

And if the "security disagios" are now rising, the replacement of an old 100% "paper value" may only be possibly with 130% new-paper-emission. If state-papers do not deliver speculative-equivalent profit, they will not be bought. Bankrupt states, at the moment, are even worse, so paying 30% on top might be right, for the moment.

But at 30% inflation-rate (on statal-papers), the "dangerous" area of "hyper-inflation and depreciation" for the "real-economy" is surpassed - and a crisis can arise. To avoid this, the ECB (European Central Bank) intervened, buying all papers. But hiding is not solving a problem. There is not much security behind the ECB. The "Euro" might lose value, with imported inflation as one of many additional problems. Or a currency-reform might be needed. The vicious-circle might continue.

The problem of too much "produced" money, un-covered debt and currency devaluations has al-ready happened once in a big scale: 1929, with very bad results in solving the problems. Sadly, to-day's politicians are seemingly unable to learn from the past. And: the actual scale is far bigger. It is only "better" hidden – at the ECB, "bad-banks" and almost new speculative-bubbles, hiding the losses of the old papers.

Unfortunately, today additional problems need to be solved - compared to 1929:

a) Since 1970, and especially since the "New Economy"-crises many bubbles have ex-ploded and many states and central banks have dramatically increased their debts: up to 300% of GDP (gross domestic product) in many developed countries. Less or more hidden.

b) If the states and banks would re-start to trust each other again, a part of the money (not yet used for speculation) might be used for and from the real economy. This "small" part of the speculative money is still a great part for the real sector, as the amount of specu-lative money is 50 to 100 times greater than the needed money at the real economy. This even could become too much money – and lead to a high commodity-inflation. But states and banks don't trust each other.

c) Inflation must be stopped by 1.) higher inter-est rates or 2.) capital restrictions. High in-terest rates, however, cannot be paid by the indebted states or banks. Neither by the weakening real economy. And capital re-strictions lead to lower money circulation and undesirable blocking of the economic growth.

d) The prescription of low interest rates by the central banks (so that governments are able to service their debts) causes problems in other sectors: 1.) Insurance companies that have expected higher average interest rates. They get problems when insurance contracts with guaranteed high interest rates must be phased out and paid out. As a result, insurances had to get state aid as well. 2.) The Banks are unwilling to lend to "real-economy" if the risk cannot be secured by higher interest rates. If interest rates are lower than potential profits from speculation, speculation will absorb all the money.

e) The cash flow problems from the above-mentioned constellations prompted large companies to widen their payment terms on the purchasing side: up to three months later. Additionally, they reduced the timeframe of their claims from their sales by three months and/or even required advance payment. To the detriment of their - primarily - smaller business partners. And: if now primarily the small (at first glance: politically not significant) companies become insolvent, then unemployment is on the increase, as small firms account for around 80% of the population employment.

f) Consumption - as a possible growth stimulator - is currently not increasing. Consumers are the main losers from current trends: 1.) You get no interest paid for their savings. 2.) The surplus in earnings at expiring insurance contracts was abolished (as part of the deal) when the state "rescued" the insurance companies . 3.) Wealth fades, as a lot of money got lost due to mis-consulting and mis-speculation. 4.) Jobs disappear because companies need to save money. 5.) Planning for future is made more difficult, with only short-term employees-contracts.

g) Until now, major security disagios for state/bank and corporate securities could be avoided, as central banks gave guarantees or bought the securities under "usual" conditions. But: the higher the debt, the higher the risks. As well resulting from central bank activities.

h) The legal uncertainty about 1.) bad-banks 2.) all-paper purchases of central banks and 3.) all those bubbles flying around may lead to an increased general mistrust. Trust is one of the main value-aspects behind everything. If trust switches to distrust, all bubbles will explode. We will get a big crise.

i) (Virtual) Money has lost a lot of trust. The value-preservation and exchange-guarantee functions of the money are damaged. And with them: the functionality of the money cycle as such.

j) Actually all economy systems have become very vulnerable. Re-acting, not pro-acting. Incapable of switching to something new. Not being able to stop the vicious circle. Not being able to really address new challenges, as sustainability aspects, urgently needed. We urgently need a change. Otherwise this vulnerability will lead to a big crisis. At any aspect coming as new challenge. From wherever: Climate, epidemies, mistrust …

It is time to reflect on the current theoretical macro-economy models before tackling new alternative solutions:

E. Money: a central aspect in most of the important economic theories

In the book "Astron-Economy-Solutions" we presented "money" as a cycle parallel to the cycle of goods and services - but called it "exchange medium". One of the new key questions is: Is "money" (as it is today) really needed in an economic cycle?

Humanity has always traded. There have always been suppliers of goods and services in many sectors who exchanged their goods and services for the goods and services of another supplier.

The exchange processes in previous times were a little bit more complicated. Sometimes a goat had to be exchanged for 4 geese at a market stand, before 2 of the geese could be exchanged against a needed knife. The remaining 2 geese could now be exchanged for other things.

In these old times money was not really needed. And no one would have trusted "paper". And people had time to exchange. And the variety of things they needed was small. And all the goods needed could be exchanged at only one market.

When the world got wider, the goods offered increased and time as such became an important factor. Many different exchange media were invented: shells, beads, silver, gold, copper coins with imprinted values (higher than the metal value), paper money (value like coin-system) and virtual money: money was born.

But although exchange media and money existed since long time, the first economy-theory including money as an exchange-medium in a cycle appeared very late: in the middle of the 18th century.

1. The Physiocrats - Francois Quesnay

Francois Quesnay published the first economy book at all in 1758. It included a model of money circulating parallel to the circulating goods and services. As a doctor, he compared things to correlations in the blood circuits.

2. The Classic - Adam Smith, Th. Malthus, J. B. Say, D. Ricardo, J. St. Mill ...

In the decade of 1770, the first great classical model by Adam Smith was published: "An Inquiry to the Nature and Causes of the Wealth of Nations." In it: the "invisible hand" of the price mechanism.

3. The Neoclassical - W. Jevons, C. Menger, L. Walras, A. Marshall

In the 1930s, the power of individuals in the economy was discovered and the microeconomic aspects such as marginal costs and - benefits that can influence decisions. Prices were no longer calculated on a cost basis. They now were adapted on the respective willingness to pay.

4. Keynesianism - J.M. Keynes

1936 Keynes published the book "General Theory of Employment, Interest and Money". He removed from micro-economy towards macro-economy. Its introduction of the state demand policy to reduce unemployment was successful only once. Lamentably it was the beginning of the endless indebtedness of all states.

5. The Monetarists - M. Friedman

A counter-theory to Keynes began in the 1960s and gained in importance in the 1970s. It focused on supply rather than demand policy. And money regulation as the main instruments for economic stability.

There are far more theories. But all the important ones everyone are build on - and trusts in - money.

6. AstronTimeOnomy - Albert Bright

"Time is money"? – OK: "Money, be it time"!

New ideas, theories and models always have a hard time being accepted and implemented. In all areas - even in "technical" astronomy. When Albert Einstein presented his ideas, many physicists even founded an association called "100 German Physicists against the theories of Einstein". Einstein's reaction: "If they were right, one physicist would have sufficed." Let´s try with new ideas about money …

Lamentably none of the "established" economy-theories of the actual "status quo" has a solution against all those bubbles and vicious-circles that have emerged in the past decades. And on the basis of all those theoretical models of capital-rules not even mutual break-through-decisions and visions of the United Nations (193 states as members) can be achieved. 5 years after the 17 UN-SDGs (17 United Nations Sustainable Development goals) not even the first and most important one (no poverty) has been - not even partly - been achieved. The actual situation is even worse(!) than before the UN-decision.

Capital goes own ways. No (actual) theory can stop. Nor 193 UN-States can stop. Lamentably, not even capital can stop its own way within its own vicious circle. If all wealth is concentrated at 1%, no one will be able to buy the products and services of capital. Capital collapses.

As to Albert Einstein: "You can´t solve a problem with the same tools, which lead to it!"

New ways are required! Why not "astronomy for economy".

It would be conducive to economy, if the ideas of

Brights book, AstronZeitOnomy (2014) would be introduced. This actual book you are reading - AstronTimeOnomy - is the British version of AstronZeitOnomie. It is an amplified version and connected to former and later inventions of additional formulas from Albert Bright.

Compared to all old theories, AstronZeitOnomie is the first economy theory that is no longer based on money-circuits. It is mainly based on time(-unit)-cycles. And it is based on astronomy: on Brights´ invented formula of time.

Money can be replaced by time units. Time has the same dimension in each individual country: 24 hours, 365 days, lifetime, ...

And time-unit-accounts can easily be introduced nowadays by banks or credit card companies, among others. "Time" only needs to be denominated as a new "foreign currency" in the systems.

Money has been badly missed in the past crises, since 2000 ("new economy"). At moment it is difficult to find a way out of the vicious circle without causing another kind of crisis. (That was the view when texting AstronZeitOnomie beginning of 2012). But: In the actual crisis, there seems to be too much money… (continuously "printed" and dramatically widened since 07-2012 with Draghi´s 3 words "whatever it takes"). Such quick monetary-policy-changes are difficult to handle. Specially, in the long-term investment-plans of companies. So, the additional money went to speculation, as no investment was planed in bad times …

Now, in 2019/2020, due to the corona crisis, additional money is being printed on top of all that money already produced. The actual capital-models of the past are not able to cope with all these requirements.

So, let´s go new ways. Based on new tools. Based on astronomy.

The proposed new approach is not intended to destroy money aspects, but merely to relativize them. And a new parallel world will be constructed – with time-unit(-accounts) as the new clearing basis.

F. THE ECONOMY MODEL ASTRON-TIME-ONOMY (ASTRON-ZEIT-ONOMIE)

F.1. Consideration of astronomical aspects

By adding "Astron" we want to point out that we are not just looking to replace money by time-units within the current economy-models. Other astronomical rules must also be followed in order to maximize the success of the new approach. The most important of the astronomy dimensions are "reinterpreted" as well.

Just for getting you curious: in the next books we as well will address autonomy, liberty, peace and sustainability – based on different astronomy-aspects. For example:

a) Concerning autonomy Albert Einstein discovered, that each planet optimizes its own path/ orbit autonomously. It is not a star (not a "statal-authority") in the center of a solar system, as Isaac Newton thought, which determines the orbits of its planets.

b) Concerning peace: far less collisions of systems, (less crises) are a fact in universe. This is made possible in universe as there is an (apparently) endless space-dimension. The space-formula was discovered by Albert Bright (in 2016, after publishing this actual first book ...).

This space dimension is not territorial gains as many dictators on earth always try to achieve. Extrapolated "space" in universe is energy. Therefore "energetic space" on earth can be the freedom of thinking. Brain-energy does not need space, it keeps within the dimensions of our brain and head. Thus, each individual would have a comparable freedom, by enjoying the energy of free thinking. Comparable to that freedom of the planets in space, to go(!) own ways. There is enough "space" in our brains for not colliding. Nor being restricted by - state, religion, income, gender, skin color, age .... Without being manipulated nor restricted, the brain is very open. Only paying attention to central rules of human rights and coexistence, things will go better than today. Via liberty attitudes, caring for mutual "space". Everybody for everybody.

For a central aspect of the universe, just one "simple" formula was needed. This defined the aspects of atoms up to the "border" of universe: the simple relativity of Albert Einstein. KIS - keep it simple is valid in the universe. It should also apply on our earth.

The main aspects that change in our new are money and a bonus-account.

a) Money in its present form is no longer required. Money in its present form is a thing without any corresponding thing nor dimension in universe. Money in its present form is a human illusion, based on human trust – but misused and attacked from many sides.
b) A bonus-account is used to copy another specialty of universe. Providing all the energy, that a star needs for its orbits for all its lifetime, at the beginning of its existence.

Let´s look for better solutions.

There are two astronomy formulas that are used in the new economic model of AstronTimeOnomy. To explain everything more comprehensibly, we use: 1.) The "Special" Theory of Relativity by Albert Einstein and 2.) the gravitational and centrifugal theories of Isaac Newton (instead of Einstein's gravity from the General Theory of Relativity ... Even Steven Hawking prefered to reckon with Newton – and even today Newton is applied to calculate and land on the moon and mars ...).

These 2 formulas help us explain the correlations of time – without too much considering other new aspects, which we invented. Both formulas meanwhile have been relativized or disproved – but are a good platform, to explain things step by step:
-   The gravitation/centrifugal-guidance model of

a star towards its planets orbits of Isaac Newton has been replaced by Albert Einstein´s "time/space-absorbing" powers of stars. In close correlation to those of the planets. With planets optimizing their orbits by themselves.

- We relativized this model of Einstein, as we invented the formulas of time and space as such. By doing so, no longer space/time-absorbing is "status quo". It was revolutionized by our space-formula (see our next book, with new inventions, launched 3 years later than this book with its time-focus …). With the space-formula we rectify Einstein´s "curved space".

But both formulas help us getting closer to additional ideas, which we invented far later. And help us not to overload with complexity, presenting all at once. So, we will use them to continuously get deeper.

The Special Relativity Theory Formula, $E = m * c^2$

E = Energy
m = Matter
c^2 = Squaring the constant "c", equivalent to the figure of lightspeed

has been transferred to the economic dimensions, which leads to the new wealth formula:

$$W = M * V^2$$

Where

W: Wealth
=:   Rules
M: Things done and produced by people - In-clusive aspects like raw materials etc.
V: Production speed/productivity
*:   Shows that the combination of substance AND productivity have a big impact on wealth
^{2}:   Shows that the speed/productivity has a far stronger impact on wealth than the kind of material/products that are produced.

No, there is no symbol in universe for the dimension of money that humanity uses in its current models.

And yes, we added the dimension "time". It is integrated into these formulas. It is hidden in "c" and "V". We define it as a part of "speed of light": 300.000 km (space) per SECOND (**time**).

At this place we need to do an EXCURSUS:

EXCURSUS:

At this place astronomers tend to disagree. And we are happy, that the actions mentioned above concerning time was a "no go" in astronomy. Just because it was a "no go", it was us, to be the happy ones, who discovered the formula of time. And by doing so – and thinking ahead – we discovered the formulas of space, dynamic-relativity, time- & space-correlation, as well as the disclosure of "dark matter" and "dark energy", the rectification of Einstein´s curved-space, ...

The "no go" has quite some reasons. Einstein discovered this figure by a lot of experiments and theoretical analysis. He was looking for a figure, a multiplicator, which might be valid to determine the energy out of any matter. No matter what kind of matter it is. With this multiplicator he wanted to define the maximum of energy possible in universe. The energy, which might result as the relative "other side" of his equation about matter "m" - correlations. He wanted to find something like Newtons "gravitational-constant". Not for gravitation, but for energy. He discovered the "c" to be that constant, that "singular figure". Valid for each kind of matter.

Einstein defined his multiplicator as "c^2". Knowing, that light-velocity, is the maximum of speed achievable, he can´t have thought of using "c" as a speed-dimension. Setting "c^2" as the multiplicator for his energy-formula, was a no-go for speed. At least at his time. Einstein used "c" as a "singular figure".

And "c", being defined as a "singular figure", you might not change it for nothing. The casualty of being the same figure as lightspeed does not mean, it might be used as speed. That is non-sense. It was nonsense ... .

We cross-thought. An initiated a big break-through within astronomy. In the following books we will as well analyze deeper a lot of the dimensions mentioned before. And prove, that it is possible to use "c" as well as speed.

End of the EXCURSUS.

The "matter", M, stands for all "aspects" and "exchange cycles" which are used for the production of goods and services. In a balanced case, this look as follows:

Entrepreneurs   Employees

                        Offer

                     "Goods" -
Investment   Creation &   Work
                     Compensat.

Demand

State   Private

Lamentably, in recent decades, the influence of state circuits has increased dramatically and has led to an imbalance, tending towards a dangerous "counter-formula" :

At "the other side" [*4] of our defined wealth-formula there are the formulas of gravitation and centrifugal-force – gravitation being the more "dangerous" one, in our Astronomy-for-Economy-Model, GobalOnomy.

$$G = y * (m1 * m2) / r^2$$

G: Gravity
y: Gravitational constant
m: Matters
r: Distance of the two matters (stars/planets)

   ... and the centrifugal force is defined as

$$Z = m * w^2 * r$$

  m: Matter (planet/star)
  w: Speed of angles

r: Leverage arm

... and, in addition, it applies that

G + Z = K

Both values, G and Z added, are always constant with respect to the respective m1 (star)
and mX (planets) – within one galaxy.

These astronomy results from Newton transferred
to a new economy model lead to the following new
definitions:

G: C = Centralization Power

y: i = in-activity constant

m: b = managing instances

r: d = distance of "instances"

C = i (b1 * b2) / d²

**And there is also a centrifugal force in the
economic equivalent:**

Z: F = Centrifugal force

m: b = Governing bodies

w: a = Activity speed

r: s = distance "wish"

Absolute centralization, 1 point, no space, no speed, nothing: (s = 0 , means: F = 0), as
$$F = b * a^2 * s$$

As well in economy the sum of both forces, C and F, always is constant at the respective observed instances. The farer away from an authority, the greater the liberty.

$$C + F = K$$

It is a lot of letters. However, these will be imaginable within the following texts.

Originally, in my book "Astron-Economic Solutions" [3] I only wanted to present a new model based on Einstein's "Special Theory of Relativity". As a better model for the wealth of nations. But looking at reality, Newton's gravitational formulas could also be applied to the economy - and, lamentably, they are implemented and followed by many states.

In addition, in my first book*², I found that both (!), Einstein and Newton's formulas lead to the same amount of energy E. Newton, when his formulas are extrapolated to the mental dimensions of Einstein. These are dimensions, at which - at Newton´s times - nobody dared to think about.

Centralized states also create prosperity. In fact, they do - ostensibly. But now comes the extrapolation. Both formulas at their extremes lead to the same energy.

But the "wealth" from these energy production processes is not the same. Prosperity (with todays matter-focus) is created by the things generated with - and out of - matter:

a) **With the formula of Einstein** one possibility (which, at the beginning, was as well promoted by Stephen Hawking) of things happening, when matter is accelerated to square-light-speed was:
Close to square-light-speed, matter will get extremely hot. Heat leads to expansion. Matter might be endless (and wealth in our model as well...).

However, different aspects disproved this idea:
- c² can´t be achieved, because more energy is needed to get into the range of c² than the energy that would be generated as a result of the equation, "E=m*c²".
- c (up to our new status-quo) is the maximum speed. Using c² as speed made no sense.
- according to the generally accepted definition, the amount of energy is constant. The absolute E-status of matter is not achievable - at least not with the current know-how status.
- This is not, what we see at the end of our universe. At least not in our visible areas.

Stephen Hawking withdraw his thoughts about this idea. The arguments mentioned above were so strong, that nobody dared again, to think about velocity when talking about "c".

Nobody till us - as we were not mainly thinking about matter. We wanted more aspects to be considered (time, space…). Thus, we were the lucky ones to discovered their formulas.

And yes, with our new formulas, it makes sense to define a ("similar") formula (like that) of Einstein´s "Simple-Relativity" to be the "wealth-side" and "direction" of an astronomy-based economy-model.

b) Within the formulas of Newton, if gravity is endless (extrapolated with the dimensions of Einstein), the energy will be squeezed out of matter - and matter will collapse in a mega-nova (extrapolation of super-nova …). And if there is no matter anymore, only one point will remain, and one point is (mathematically) nothing. Thus, wealth will be destroyed. No energy maximum with (presumably) matter conservation, as with Einstein, will be generated. Instead, energy will be squeezed out of all matter, destroying the matter, absorbing the rest of it into a "black-whole".

There are two aspects concerning the circuits within and between all the aspects involved (entrepreneurs, employees, government, private, - investments, labor, supply, demand, ...) in the above overview:

The better the circulation, the larger and richer a country or a company can become.

But if one of the parts of the model becomes too large, a lot of gravity will be unfolded in this special part. It will attract much resources for itself. Then the wealth of nations will decrease or even get lost due to the emergence of unbalancing forces.

With regard to the time aspect, the following applies:

Within the wealth formula, the dimension of time is part of a squared basis. So, it is more important than matter.

Within the gravity formula, time is not represented. If only extreme central gravity-power is active, there will be no more people, companies nor institutions that try to "escape" by centrifugal force. Centrifugal force contains time as a part of its speed-dimension. So, with only gravity - and without any centrifugal force balancing the system, no time will be present anymore. Thus, a matter without (its own) time will implode. There will be a super-nova, if gravity grows too strong, pushing aside all other forces. And at a black-hole no matter will remain at all.

Too much gravity or centralization, which tries to regulate too many dimensions, usually causes the system to collapse. This also applies to the centralization and/or extremely expanding (gravity-gathering) states and politicians. History has shown time and again. And this also applies to companies that are too large (without enough "internal power" compensating): of all the companies listed 100 years ago, only less than 1% still exist today.

Time (especially in combination with speed) has an enormous influence on the function of systems. Therefore, time and its influences must be considered as a central aspect, when it comes up to generate wealth.

As time is so important and such a brilliant dimension in universe - and as money has no similar dimension nor importance in universe at all - why then, not replacing money by time on our earth? Or at least introduce as a parallel "currency" for a parallel system?

"Time is money" is a popular saying. This can easily be reversed (because it is an equation): "Money is time". And to optimize things:

"Money, be time!"

Our "Astron-Time-Onomy" model works without money. It works with international valid "time(-units)" correlated to real existing (astronomic) aspects – and not "mismanaged" by politics nor speculation…

F.2. Implementation of the Time dimension

Time should be used as a parallel currency, as "TV", Time-Valuta, and introduced by banks as an individual account for each person. As well for all companies and governments.

F.3. Creating Values

There are already many systems to count and manage time. But these systems only take up practice - and do not create any added value.

To generate a value that can be used as "energy" (= "power to do something") in order to ...

a) increasing wealth - and

b) relativize current money problems

... the idea is to give each person an individual time-value account with a large TV-time-value-quantity for individual use. This should not be accessible for banks nor state nor society. And should not be useable for speculation. By this, speculation, mis-investment and wealth losses in those tremendous dimensions as in the past decades will be avoided. Errors can thus be reduced to individual people and decisions.

This gives every human being the freedom of a "planet". Everyone will be able to optimize his own way (as Einstein discovered to be valid for planets). An own way without restrictions in time, nor money, nor institutional aspects, nor religion, nor education, etc. Only the respective central rules of the respective star-space constellations should be used for and by the "planets" to circulate around.

The rules of the state (rules of the stars), should be reduced to a minimum: to create the maximum of liberty for its inhabitants (planets). By this planets will be able to act (circulate) in their own way.

Each planet goes its own way. And together with its star, always expanding their orbits. And via this expansion they will parallel expand the universe, ever faster. This "space" (energy) expansion in the universe is comparable to prosperity, generated by "free space" of/for ideas on earth.

Stars get older. And somewhen - with relatively too little energy - they will implode. Predictable.

Our own sun, for example, is estimated to implode in about 5,000,000,000 years. But until this time it will have done an enormous work achieving space- expansion thanks to its initial energy. With this space expansion stars and planets continuously achieve more liberty. As well there will be less collisions with other systems. It, thus, is a gain in wealth.

Why not give each person his own life(-time-valuta)- "energy" (= power to do work!)? As well in the advance! Off birth. On the same way as the stars get their initial energy from the big bang. Or at later births, from dust concentrations. In this way, each person could go its own way. By this (also because of being much more motivated) far more overall wealth would be generated.

Policy, at the start of the new system, may decide whether to implement restrictions. For example: on the use of a certain maximum of the time-account per year. In order to prevent the less educated people from possibly losing (too much) wealth.

With this additional world-wide-wealth, all the current problems are put into almost nothing, to a mini-point.

The debt per person - due to speculations of private, banks and states – in 2017 was at £ 100.000. That was 400% of the average income of 25.000 £ per year. This debt could be downsized to 10% if the total life-time-valuta-income would be booked on the account of each person. If a person has an age of 25 years he has still 40 years of possible work. 40y * 25,000TV = 1.000.000TV.

Even if, at the beginning of the implementation, there are restrictions on annual expenditure, in order to prevent possible misuse, the impulse of the implementation should still lead to a "big bang". It will allow the overcoming of all the constraints that currently prevent growth, due to lack of demand. And this measure will lead to an endlessly growing "world universe". World-wide-wealth.

If everyone is wealthy, this will solve all 17 Sustainable Development Goals of United-Nations at once. And even far more aspects. Now.

And this will turn around the Maslow-Pyramid of needs. The lower steps of survival and profiling, causing a lot of rivalries and problems, will be gone.

An "investment" limit of 5% per year, within 5 years (to study, for example) leads to 50,000 TV per year, 250,000 TV for 5 years until the end of a university-study. This is sufficient to study and to provide the family with an income. If after these 5 years no - or at least no higher – income is achieved, there could be additional rules to follow. It could be a rule (for this person) according to which it is not allowed to continue to "invest" in studying for the 5 following years. Just in order to avoid more losses for this person. What precise data and rules are taken, should be a political decision. At least at the beginning of the introduction.

If no international valid decisions are possible, TV will have different values, depending on the country in which each person lives. And if someone emigrates to another country with a higher TV-wage for their profession, he will become more prosperous. The same as today.

But (even for a first implementation step, which could be limited to a minimum) this TV-system implementation will:
a) increase wealth - and
b) relativize all those current problems of the UN.

F.4. Implementation-aspects

In the past, there were not enough technical ways to manage TV-accounts for all companies and every person in this world.

Today this is possible.

4.1. TV-(Time-Valuta)-accounts

4.1.1. Technical ways

a. time accounts instead of, or parallel to money

Switching from "money" towards TV is very simple: the banking sector (among others) only needs to introduce a new "currency"-value/variable, parallel to all existing currencies: "Time": TV

b. TV-accounts for working time

Time recording systems are nothing unusual anymore. Nowhere in the world.

c. Time accounts for life-time

There are a lot of institutionalized systems for time recordings within various official documentation authorities. From birth certificates to death certificates. We are timed. Every day of our lives. And there are official statistics of the achievable average age of people. At different sides of this world. In most of the developed countries, the average lifetime can also be differentiated by gender, job type, lifestyle ...

Therefore, it is possible to predict an average

lifetime for each person. Everywhere.

4.1.2. Wealth aspects

a) Macroeconomic aspects

Even without being introduced immediately. This model gives the perspective that all the bad banks and other bubbles may be handled without damage to the rest of the world economy and wealth.

b) Microeconomic aspects

Any person and company can be paid or pay in a currency or in TV-units.

Within the new TV-dimensions, "matter"-aspects no longer have much focus. Nor do all that "virtual"-money-aspects with all their actually misleading tendencies.

| I think, so I am | living |
| I live, so I have | time |

"Time is money"? Ok: "Money, be time!"

The world has changed from matter-property to

financial-property. Now it's time to change to TV.

4.1.3. Last not least

For many people money in our world is like the light in universe. But light only is relevant at 0.4% aspects of universe: iridescent stars. Money illuminates the value of goods and services - and helps to assess the GDP of countries. But money, more and more, just is dazzling. Tremendously bright. So bright that we hardly are able to see anything at all anymore. And light that has no purpose anymore, only dazzles, it is worth nothing. Especially when no one can be blinded any more. And the more people look away, the more the value will fall. And if no one cares, it may continue to fly around the world, but people will focus on alternative ideas: We suggest "TV". Time is closer to astronomical rules and dimensions than the artificially constructed "money". Money does not exist as a counterpart in astronomy.

Time is much closer to light than money. And it does not dazzle.

The lifetime of people is an experience and cannot be manipulated. At least not in the way it happens with money.

In addition, entrepreneurs may dispose from an TV-company-account. This may consider as additional value the quantity of people they employ. The value might be a kind of bonus for investment. And the value of this bonus on the account might be increased depending on what they do for society. Turnover or profit can be used in various ways to be transferred to this account. And all bonuses could be considered for times when an error occurs. This error-damage would then be deducted from the plus of the account. In any case: there is far more buffer in the new system than with the current capital constrained systems.

Yes, there are many new political and economic rules that need to be implemented. And, as with previous money, each country can pursue less or more successful policies. But the new freedom gained for individuals and businesses will lead to huge wealth gains.

And in our human-oriented world-model, it will no longer be the centralized capital, which dominates. The new energy or power (to do work) is applied to all and every single person and company. And the sum of all of them within a country or company will trigger a new great wave of growth and wealth. And this wealth will be kept more crisis-resistant. In a more sustainable way.

In this model there will be more opportunities for each person. And also for companies and countries. And many ideas which so far have been blocked because of money shortages now can be implemented. The past money shortages caused by mismanaging of money at a lot of institutions and government sectors will no longer be possible in the new system.

4.2. Rules and recommendations

Of course, as in all other economic models, there must also be rules for the Astron-Time-Onomy model to avoid chaos.

Therefore, the first rules are presented below, which, however, still have to be adapted politically in each country.

4.2.1. Personal life-work time

The first aspect of the model is the definition of a person's expected average life-time - adapted to the specificities that apply to the respective citizens. Let's set the average human working-lifetime at 50 years.

4.2.2. Personal life work time bonus

The second central aspect of this model is that each person receives a personal start-capital at birth. Thus, no one will be restricted, neither by parental income, social class, political nor religious aspects. And everyone is able to establish himself. Depending on his commitment.

The seed capital in figures:

50 years * 365 days = 18,250 time-bonus

4.2.3. Personal life-work-time-valuta TV

"TV". The third aspect of this model takes into account the realities of the various regions of the world: average incomes. Depending on where someone is born, the start bonus "TV", may differ. But every person will be able to change his or her place of life - if politics allows it. And this change also adjusts their "TV". However, the new prosperity reduces the migration urge to a minimum. Everyone is rich and happy in his surroundings

4.2.3.1. Income in top industry countries: 25.000
18.250 * 25.000 = 456.250.000 TV

4.2.3.2. Income in pre-industry countries: 15,000
18,250 * 15,000 = 273,750,000 TV

4.2.3.3. Income in developing countries: 5,000
18,250 * 5,000 = 91,250,000 TV

4.2.4. Consumption and Savings

The theoretically easiest way to get your own TV increase is emigrating from a low developed country to a more developed country. But at least for now: This is the most difficult way in reality. And it becomes less necessary with our model.

A second possibility would be for a family to increase its TV by having more children. This is not possible in China due to political restrictions. But there should be restrictions as well for the use of the TV of the newborn child. The use of this TV should be restricted to services aspects for the newborn child. These may be aspects, such as food, health, clothing, education. No risks nor own enriching with this TV should be allowed. Otherwise the child would be deprived of his TV.

4.2.4.1. Life starts with consumption

The start TV of each newborn child will be added to an administrator account of the parents. Depending on the average cost of living and education in the country, the child TV account bonus will be reduced from month to month.

The focus here is on the children's account - and no longer on the parents' account, as currently is the case in most countries.

Until adulthood, it will be primarily consumption that characterizes this account. Work should not be allowed before reaching the age of majority. Because education is the most important source of long-term prosperity. Children should not be abused for work by their parents in order to achieve a short-sighted higher family income for the parents. Up to the age of majority, a quarter of the tempus could be consumed: for example: 100,000,000 TV in industrialized countries.

4.2.4.2. Parents Compensations

In dependency of the policy of the region or of a

country, an additional remuneration may be awarded to the parents. This is plausible, as at least one of them will work less. This is a political decision of the respective country and could lead to more or less wealth. Most likely however, such measures will no longer be required in the long term.

4.2.4.3. Adults

With adulthood, the first main decision must be taken by the ex-teenager. Continue to consume by studying, in order to achieve a higher education and better salary in the future? Or alternatively, take up work and live at an average wage-level. The point is that both options are possible without having to resort to the income of the family, nor depend on subsidy measures of the policy.

When studying in another country, the TV is adjusted to the medium content of that country. In the interest of mutual benefit. The host country can be interested in winning students. It may get TV from his TV account for university costs. As well it will possibly benefit from a good worker in the future. The student can live with the higher costs in this country and may gain the knowledge of what he wanted. Most possibly afterwards he will get a higher salary. And pay higher taxes, after his studies, when working.

4.2.4.4. Cumulative value aspects:

Of course, each person can and should save a bonus above the start TV capital bonus.

The income set for political, charitable or voluntary work can be a political decision. And since charitable volunteers make a contribution to society, a bonus should be given as well for charitable engagement. Means, not as now: nothing. Charging all the community in order to finance this bonus is easier than now, as everyone is rich. And being transcendent (Maslow-Pyramid-Peak) will ease things additionally. The TV model makes this possible parallel to capital model constructions. Without having to consider all the non-running aspects.

A calculation of the additional-value aspects of all criteria can be as follows:

a) Birth	TV-start-bonus
b) Education	Subtraction
c) Working hours p.a.	Multiplication w. d)
d) (Salary/hour) x worktime	Addition
e) Taxes paid at lifetime	Addition

| f) Social securities payed | Addition |
| g) Donations | Addition |

If a person becomes unemployed or needs to supplement skills or takes a sabbath year, they can be rewarded during this period by means of institutionalized (without "permission bureaucracy") average income, which results from the above calculation. In this way, each individual orientates himself. Without losing social status, without "falling deep".

4.2.5. Countries

The tasks of all governments should be reduced to an absolute minimum. For the maximum of freedom for their people.

As in the universe, each planet optimizes its own path (according to Einstein). On Earth, definitely (almost) every person is able to do this. And should be allowed to go its own way. Everywhere.

No more state interventions nor (manipulated) trend- nor target-setting. And state-owned enterprises should no longer be allowed. Otherwise competition will be manipulated. Inside and outside the countries.

The main objectives of the state are:

a) Freedom for its People
b) Implementation of the same opportunities or self-determination for everyone
c) Achieving the best possible living-together, via liberty, peace and security
d) Education for self-employment
e) Education towards transcendency
f) **Sustainability**

These are very old ideals. They are based on one of the greatest strides towards increasing prosperity in humanity: The French Revolution: a) Liberté, b) Égalité, c) Fraternité.

Deplorably, states have interfered too much in everyone's lives and decisions. And the over-focus on money and capital regulation has prevented much of a possible wealth rise in the past.

With the new focus on TVs, the current money problems are put to a minimum. At the same time, the additional opportunities must be used to reduce government influence on people's and businesses' lives.

Since everyone and businesses will receive a large TV budget, neither parents nor banks nor politics are needed to "approve" much. No fights for re-distribution are needed any more. They are needed for many other things. Such as accounting for TV accounts. But no longer for arrangements or permissions. And they should be banned from speculating with the new values. Neither politicians nor banks are able to predict the forces of the markets. Time has shown time and again. And: the world is becoming even more and more complex!

The chances and risks must be reduced to the smallest possible points. In the universe to every single planet. On earth to every single person.

And in this way, the potential damage of a wrong decision is reduced to a minimum: to individuals.

There are no banks nor politics in the universe. There are only forces that compete against each other. Within just a couple of rules. There is no intervention on such a large basis like states and banks are doing on earth. This may be one of the reasons why the universe already exists 13,8 billion years. And has grown up to a 50 billion light-years diameter. And is growing faster than ever before. So: free way for the "earthly planets and stars". Without interventions which only have caused imbalances.

In order to ensure that this balance of power remains truly free and stable and cannot be manipulated by politics, the possibility of state intervention should be regulated by very stringent laws.

To ensure (a) Liberté (b) Égalité and (c) Fraternité by states, states should have the possibility of a minimal(!) taxation. The amount required for these goals depends on the constellations - and is a political decision. It will depend on the will of the people. Expressed by the majorities, through elections. And for big (regional) decisions, opinion polls should be a must. Only by drastically reducing all paternalism, the introduction of an individually available TV budget can achieve (a) Liberté, (b) Égalité and (c) Fraternité – and lead to (d) Réalisabilité.

Instead of effective taxation of up to 80% of income, a maximum of 5% should be ok. Government engagements and spending now must to be based on private decisions and initiatives. The current "care" (election promises that can only be realized with debt) of politicians now can focused towards real "wants".

TVs are calculated for each service offered by the state. But they must be competitive services. At a competitive TV. And since every person has a much larger TV budget than the money they had with previous wages in earlier times, each person has far more choice. And can choose between private and statal service.

A perfect example of this "new" freedom is the example of the French motorways. They are private and in order to use them, every user has to pay. They are in perfect condition and repaired far faster than those that are looked after by the state. Looking at the roads and bridges that are looked after by the German state, you have to say that 80% of them are dilapidated – and repairing always takes far more time and money than in France.

The solution? A far-reaching suppression of statal interference in the economy, companies or private aspects.

Recommendations: Selling German roads to private investors. And the same with the airport of Berlin, the Nürburgring, Stuttgart train-station, the railways, electricity companies, gas companies, telecommunications, aircraft, (state) car stocks, regional banks and savings banks, social housing, social security (since each person can secure itself with his own TV)

... . If state interventions in "property" is privatized, wealth will rise sharply.

The state should primarily promote liberalization. Only a minimum of taxes is required for this.
For clarity, here is a possible implementation and comparison of the valutas "time" (TV) and "money":

a) Top developed country:
TV / Person: 456.250.000 TV
Population: 64 million (United Kingdom)
GNP: 64 * 456.250.000 = 29,200,000 billion TV
Divided by 50 years: 584,000 billion GNP p.a.
(Today's GNP: 2,678 billion US $)

b) Medium developed country
TV / Person: 273,750,000 TV
Population: 1,300 million (China)
GNP: 1.300*273.750.000=355,875,000 billion TV
Divided by 50 Years: 7.117.500 Billion GNP p.a.
(Today's GNP 2,532 billion US $)

c) Low developed country
TV / Person: 91.250.000 TV

Population: 26 million (Ghana)
GNP: 26 * 91.250.000 = 2,372,500 billion TV
Divided by 50 Years: 47.50 billion p.a.
(Today's GNP: 16 billion US $)

The TV per person, of course, will vary, depending on the real life-work-time. So, this will be one of the most important goals of the states, what needs to be improved. Thus, in the future states will be looking more on individual prosperity - and less on capital in order to increase wealth …

The relation with money vs. TV between Gb, Ch and Gh is as follows:

	Gb	: Ch	: Gh
Relation-figures today	51	: 48	: 0,3
TV-based relation-figures:	7	: 92	: 0,6

The potential and the chance to increase wealth will be very great, especially for the poorer (money base) regions, if TV is introduced as a new base. TV is a far better basis as it can be used - without having to ask "central international institutions" for permission or resources. "Resources" and "capacities", which the institutions often do "not have", due to "other priorities".

From this TV-based income, the state should be

able to finance its goals and tasks - via minimal taxation.

Changing the basis from money to TV leads to a reduction in the current 300% money-based over-indebtedness. At industrialized countries this will remain at almost only 1,5%. And in China at just 0.1%. This allows politicians to act independently of the aspects of money-based theories and rules.

At the same time, statal taxation of actually 80% (direct and indirect taxation) should be reduced to a maximum of 5% in the first step. This is enough, to implement changes. But if everything has changed and much more private responsibilities and decisions are possible, then taxation should be aimed at 1% of citizens TV.

The new type of calculation will give developing country governments over-proportionate opportunities to act – as well in comparison to the developed countries. This is due to the consideration of - and focusing on - the most valuable aspects: people! – and not mainly capital.

And yes, less developed countries need this competitive advantage of relatively larger amounts of TV as: 1) they need to make most of the changes so that their citizens can compete on an international basis – and since 2) dealing with these new dimensions is more difficult to implement in less developed countries.

4.2.6. Companies

A.) General aspects

To get away from dependence on current money-based financial institutions, companies should be given a special status in a similar way to the states – depending on the workers they employ.

The summation of all their employees-TV and then starting with 2% of this value p.a., should enable each company to make all necessary changes. After the changeover period, companies' "TV-bonus" opportunities should be at around 1%, like the future taxes from states.

This "TV-bonus" should apply for each company. This gives all companies in the world the same means of accessing "finances". No matter where they are and what they produce. No matter how big or small they are. This general possibility should provide a good basis for the launch of a fair, not subsidized, non-politically supported, free economy.

In this way, no more assets are destroyed by the

misleading political interactions. The latter have always led to the misallocation of resources via incorrect prioritization.

When a company has problems, they are limited to one company and no longer to all citizens when politics tries to rescue.

And there will be no longer a "too-big-to-fail" since the state no longer has the target nor the budget nor the necessity to intervene. And states will no longer intervene in money-politics leading to mis-speculations on all sides.
Speculation should be prohibited or extremely limited. Speculation always has an egoistic focus. And all bests aim against the rest. One wins - all lose. Investment is a "give and take" and aims at a better general wealth – all win.

   B.) The TV value of companies.

The (real) company values (for society – and not for speculation) might be determined by various alternative (additional) aspects. These aspects should be: 1) outside of the stock market values, since these are no longer the real values due to 50+ times more speculative capital than real capital; 2) away from the short-term-view of speculation and 3) independent of political interests, such as "too big to fail".

The following aspects could be added:

a)   Years of Existence

The years of a company's existence is one aspect of determining the value of a company. It shows that customers and suppliers trust these products and services. This dimension can be considered and applied as a "trust bonus". Should the markets suddenly change, and the company needing investment "capital" to adapt - an institutionalized confidence bonus per year is a good tool to avoid a crisis and stabilize value. This buffer as well might help for socially acceptable dismantling in the worst case.

b)   Contribution to the Society

The contribution to society during its existence is a predictable value of a company. Of course, all (former) subsidies must be deducted from the amount of the contribution. This contribution should be calculated, considering different aspects with different "values". In addition to today's assessments, the following aspects might be considered:

(b1) Number of workers/employees

The more people, the higher a company's trust buffer value should be calculated. An "automatism" (without long-lasting and bureaucratic procedures and uncertainties, as in today's banking and government financing systems) could determine an intermediate loan for adjustment, when markets change quickly. With calculable and quickly enablement. In this way, prosperity can be better preserved than today.

(b2) Paid salaries

To engage required employees, employer must pay a certain TV on top of the basic-TV-bonus of the people. The higher the qualification, the higher the multiplier. The salaries paid in all the years of existence are a top parameter for assessing the social contribution of a company in terms of consumption tax, salary-based taxes, …

(b3) Hours worked

There are a lot of companies and organizations that provide volunteer jobs and trainings. By doing so they provide great social benefits. And: many non-profit organizations could not exist without volunteers. But yes, they provide a lot of aspects, that are very important for society. The "hours worked" are not considered in todays GNP. But "just" the hours worked do not lead to value at todays´ capital markets.

In today's limited capital markets, these companies and organizations are hardly able to obtain credit. Nor can these organizations pay their volunteers. Otherwise their business- or wealth-models would collapse.

On the other hand, there is an enormous number of people who work for "nothing" and/or often at low income levels. But make a huge contribution to society through their charitable commitment.

If a TV-"wage"-for charitable engagement would be introduced, these people would at least earn some additional wage to their base-TV in a human and respectful way to honor their commitment. This TV-wage would not come "out of nowhere" as with virtual money (for speculation aspects). Its´ basis are really worked hours and for society contribution. Thus, society may pay via redistribution. Society for society. Not one against all.

Additionally, charities will benefit from more people that really want to commit and work with them. And they now will have an additional income which leads to additional commitment and time available. And humanity will benefit from a broader support from charitable and non-profit institutions. And, despite being rich, a lot of people will continue to need help. In many sectors: education in all aspects and areas, illnesses, pandemics, etc.

By this, charities will be evaluable for GNP.

(b4) Taxes paid

Net taxes (deducting previous subsidies) which have been paid by the companies, helped society. Therefore, humanity should also be willing to help a company once it may be in need. As well this may be limited, depending on the previous deposits.

(b5) Paid social security

Since companies contribute to the general social security system, their payments as well should play a role, if once they should be in need.

(B6) Subtraction of subsidies

Subsidies must be deducted from the trust bonus account, as the respective company has already used (once) company funds.

(b7) Subtraction of state employees

If a company or model should rely on state employees, their salaries, should be deducted from a possible support.

(b8) Subtraction of State shareholdings

If a state gets involved in a company its involvement must be deducted from the trust bonus before potential assistance is payed.

(b9) Subtraction of state interventions

Special state permits such as "loss reduction measures" in the form of "bad banks", or "tax allowances", lead to a privileged position. These sums must be deduced from a potential confidence bonus before further aid-money flows. State-aid, have unfortunately, all too often, led to misallocation of resources.

c) Miscellaneous

The introduction of the TV-value for companies not only shows how important a company really is for society, compared to others that have only a "political value".

It, as well, will show us that wealth can be built primarily through appropriate work. And not mainly through donations, subsidies and re-distri-butions as low % of what "remains". And it will show us on what to concentrate in a crisis. And prevent us from investing money in unproductive sectors. Instead of investing in sectors, which are more urgently needed. As a result, a worsening of the situation on both sides - and an accelerated downward spiral - can be prevented.

With the introduction of a TV-buffer value for com-panies, bankruptcies – and thus wealth losses – will be reduced. When markets change and "money" is suddenly needed, the buffer can be used for adjustments. Relying on non-functioning banking and government systems is not needed any more. This is even more important, as, in a crisis, banks a the first to leave the platform. And states today have the possibility of "revaluating" all at once in "their" country – and destroy a lot of wealth.

In addition, much more people will take the step towards self-employment, as the risks are much lower due to 1.) elimination of the big uncertainty factors with "banks" or "states"; 2. the TV-bonus is free accessible; and 3. the buffer might help in problem times.

Both aspects, fewer bankruptcies and more entrepreneurs will lead to a great wave of additional wealth. Worldwide.

And the reducing of state activities to an absolute minimum as well will lead to more wealth, as private companies make everything cheaper faster and better.

Compare your earlier price-experiences. The times when many sectors were handled by the state. Compared with today's prices. You will get an impression of the possible wealth wave that could arise if there were more private possibilities within aviation, electricity, water, education, construction, telephone, post, state banks, state insurance (pension, health insurance, ...), employment offices ... If everything were privatized, better and cheaper products and services would result. And far less taxes and / or re-distributions would be needed!

Profitability will still play a major role. But if all companies only produce with machines without anyone employed, no one will be able to buy what is produced. At least not within the actual capital rules. That is why, a humanitarian company TV-value should be introduced as a ranking so that consumers can assess which product they really want to buy. Which company they want to promote.

4.2.7. Employees / citizens

Within the GlobalOnomy model each citizen of this world will get a "Working-Life-Time-Units-Basic-Bonus". They will get it at birth - like stars get their – main - life-time-energy at their start. It may – in the first step – depend on the average lifetime and average lifetime-income. But everybody on earth will be – relative - rich. All the 17-UN-SDGs (17 United Nations Sustainable Development Goals) can be achieved at once. With just this one step within the GlobalOnomy model. And the missing "demand" within our present economy-crisis will be established. On a stable basis. And relativizing all actual bubbles to a minimum.

There are other models trying to solve some of the actual problems. But their basis is not so strong as our GlobalOnomy-Model. And their focus is too focused, not global.

For example, there are various organizations working for a first step of a guaranteed and unconditional basic income. This is a good step towards the general integration of all citizens into a humane and dignified social environment. But these organizations stand as supplicants and competitors to many other companies and institutions, which also want a part of the limited money.

These organizations are losing against their capital "competitors". In the capital systems, ROI, return on investment, counts. And social aspects are only considered at a low level. Just to prevent against a revolution.

Additionally, a "basic income" is just a minimum basic "wage". Those profiting from that minimum wage, will continue to be dependent on the profitability and re-distribution-capacity of the state. As well on different parties. And on mayorities possibly changing after elections.

With that minimum, they will not be able to go own ways - as in our GlobalOnomy-model. They will vegetate in a poor existence. At the lowest steps of Maslow´s pyramid-of-needs. Our model tends to elevate all mankind to the top of that Maslow pyramid: towards "empathy" and "transcendency" (in its´ non-religious meaning). Doing good things (see later).

The basic-income model will not really increase demand, as needed. Poor people only buy cheap products. To produce cheap, companies need to automize. Automating leads to job-cuts. Job-cuts lead to low social payments. Low income leads to less demand and lower prices. One of the actual vicious circles.

Distributing limited capital towards another, new re-distribution (basic-income) within rich industrialized countries leads to less capital for developing purposes. Developing countries, need that money far more extremely than "poorer" people in rich countries. Therefore basic-income is a quite egoistic movement and no solution for the real problems of this world.

Poor countries – in todays´ capital systems – will not be able to pay their citizens a basic-income. Poverty - and all of the 17 United Nations Sustainable Development Goals - will remain or even get worse, as additional money will be withdrawn towards rich countries "requirements".

"TV", in contrast, can(!) change the world. And therefor it should be introduced parallel(!) to all capital- & money-based markets / models.

People will have much more choice to do what they really like, as their lives are financed through their own (!) bonus.

People do not depend on the "good will" of other decision-makers.

An additional "foreign currency account" (for TV) with far less rules than those of the current capital markets, can also be introduced "institutionally" far faster than the "(unconditional) basic income" models.

Potentially, there is no un-employment anymore. Nor need for re-distribution. No artificial "constructions" must invented, in order to reduce (hide) unemployment. No basic-income re-distribution is required. Politics can concentrate on central aspects.

Companies will probably have to pay higher salaries, as workers now have more freedom of choice. Of doing own things. Going own ways. On the other hand, however, companies can be sure that the people who then work for them, really want to work for them. And will generate a much higher productivity. Income in general rises due to 1) the higher wages (from companies); 2) the larger wage-basis (due to the additional salaries at charitable institutions, etc.) and 3) as well due to rich population (general TV-bonus for all humanity). This leads to more worldwide demand. Entrepreneurs will benefit ahead of paying higher wages.

4.2.8. Entrepreneurship

"Companies" and "self-employed" should be able to build and use their own "existence" PV-bonus without any restrictions

In each country there are averages of company existence times - and of their turnovers and employees, over the years.

In order to stimulate economy and employment not only the actual quantity of employees should be considered for the TV-value of a company. In order to promote entrepreneurship, companies should in addition be compassed with the average lifetime (years) of companies in the respective country, as one of the multipliers for their value. The same approach as with the bonus account for each individual! This is a big point for policymakers to treat all companies relatively equal. As well, it optimizes the entrepreneurs´ chances of survival in general (!) – without focusing on only the large companies, as in todays´ capital economy.

In universe not: "too big to fail" is valid – but: "too big to survive" applies. It is one of the reasons for "super-nova"-implosions – and the loosing of all matter of stars and their surrounding planets.

This will not only make it possible for far more people to realize their ideas and dreams. This will increase wealth in total. It will also encourage governments to introduce the best infrastructure to help businesses arise: liberty (!) – the liberty of the universe, where each stars and planets optimize their own orbits (as to Albert Einstein).

And since all companies and all people count, states will compete against each other for gaining people with ideas and entrepreneurship. The liberating of barriers for people to immigrate to the country, no matter where they come from, will advance. And the internationalization of humanity will increase enormously. Politically or religiously set barriers are reduced. "Help" will be prioritized instead of the current "ignorance".

The calculations for entrepreneurs can be made as before for the companies.

In order to reward the success of existing entrepreneurs and their companies, there must be an appreciation for the years of their existence. In addition to the average, which benefits the new start-ups. Each year of its existence could be "benefitted" with 1% of the corresponding employees-TV of the corresponding year.
After 100 years, a company will have 100% of the

tempus of its employee tempus. As an additional tempus bonus. With this, companies can invest - or if critical, this bonus can be used for restructuring and realignment. Therefore, no longer only 1% of companies listed 100 years ago (at Wallstreet) will "still exist" today. Most probably it will be 99% "still existing". And it is no longer speculative capital evaluating. But it will be the most important factor of all: people, mankind involved.

These models are as well applicable to secure creditors. When a company goes bankrupt, the buffer can be used for socially acceptable dismantlement. And no entrepreneur is treated badly for bankruptcy anymore. But will rather be encouraged to start something new. And creditors will suffer only minor, if any, damage.

It are the entrepreneurs which added wealth to this world in the past. If their companies fail, the previous contribution to wealth must be considered.

With the TV-based model of GlobalOnomy, all these aspects are implementable. A lot easier as in the money-based capital-world.

There will no longer be just a small number of big

"money owners" and big entrepreneurs, which determine the destiny of the world. But it will be all mankind as entrepreneurs, using their TV-bonus.

Current money-based entrepreneurs and investors, on the other hand, will not lose their money and investments. All values are retained. No debt reduction, no currency devaluation nor property "redistribution" will take place. "Only" their relative "share" of wealth decreases, compared to the new TV possibilities of all human TV-bonuses. And because people have far more liberty and tremendous (demand-)power, entrepreneurs now need to focus more on people - than on money or capital in the past.
Actual wealth and property will only remain, if their proprietors are able to inspire people for themselves, and for their businesses. They may no longer just impose their own ideas based on capital-power. A lot more social aspects must be taken into account. A great social change.

Entrepreneurship will be easy(er), as people may invest for example 25% of their TV within 5 years wherever they want. They may decide to become self-employed far easier than today.

4.2.9. Failures

If a business does not work, its entrepreneurs will not fall into a deep hole. The company has stored enough TV to balance the claims and interests of all parties involved. Entrepreneurial energy as such is thus maintained, and new ventures can arise. Now, on the basis of more experience.

Entrepreneurial energy is what the world needs to generate wealth. Failures should be seen as a learning process to make it better next time. "Making it better" is one of the central aspects that a society must promote. And not the condemnation of those who have been unlucky.

The Spanish "No hay mal, que por bién no venga!" ("there is no bad, that does not come for good!") must be internalized. We should positively and optimistically use as well the bad (experience), to improve the world.

Every child must learn from mistakes. And, despite many mistakes, children are not declassified or condemned. But they are being helped and promoted forward.

The importance of every single company must and can be put into perspective with the TV and the new theory. And the capacity of society to compensate failures can be dramatically increased with the TV-bonus-model: Towards the level of "caring parents" who repeatedly encourage children to become self-employed (and not to become dependent, as in many current economic models). This is a huge step forward, compared to the focus of the limited money/capital available. We can relativize these limitations, which we (!) have imposed ourselves(!) with the money/capital ideas/models. We can relativize all the past with the new ideas/models. We just need to "just do it".

Of course, there might be restrictions on the quantity of trials. The systems as well may differ from country to country, depending on cultures and the status of development. But the governments with the best re-funding solutions - as opposed to current restrictions - will achieve the greatest success.

4.2.10. Welfare- /non-profit-organizations

Welfare work is perfect for fulfilling many general activities which earlier have been done by families, churches and states.

Welfare engagements are not only good for the (international) help for people and projects in need. Since welfare-engagements usually act absolute neutrally, their interventions are more tolerated than statal or ecclesiastical interventions, behind which often, additional interests are hidden.

That so many people are ready to spend their time for good causes, shows people's desire to do something positive. And it is a proof that most people will not be lazy if TV-bonus-accounts will become effective(!).

As well the fact, that so many people donate to these organizations shows the great respect and broad recognition of the importance of these organizations. The step to affirm a payment - the oversight with a TV-bonus for all of those committed people - is very a very small one ...

4.2.11. Church and similar organizations

Churches and similar organizations give help and hope to all those people who believe in their ideas. The "energy" they provide is a primarily mental energy.

Since tempus will be a mental "payment surrogate", its introduction within churches should be easily possible. As well because churches do not have so much things to buy and sell - as companies have - in order to pay their committed people.

4.2.12. Educational institutions

Schools, universities & Co. have an enormous value for achieving wealth. And their values and services will increase dramatically if people own a TV-bonus. Many recipients will invest in better education. Higher demand will lead to higher supply, more teachers, more knowledge and wisdom. And increased wealth. Automatically. No state intervention is required. Competition - and not the authorities - will set the standard.

4.2.13. The "doing-nothing"

Free weekends, holidays, disease-recovery-times, sabbath years, pensioners, un-employment - all that "doing-nothing" that humanity has implemented in the past, it should and can continue in future as well. And even with less stress.

But the people who are undergoing the system - consciously or not - must be accompanied. Some people could be "blinded" by the large amount of TV. They need to understand that TV "only" is a bonus on their future, which they can use to optimize themselves. But "doing nothing at all" will damage them, sooner or later.

In order to get this model to bear fruit, it is essential that the state no longer has any influence on the pension system. Because if the pension funds are used politically for other purposes, of course no one has confidence in the pension payment-ability of the state. This is happening time and again. If doing-nothing leads to the same income-result as in the low-wage-sector, "vulnerable people" will choose to do nothing. And prefer to live on the basis of social assistance instead of working "hard". A self-inflicted political failure.

"Slacker" (doing-nothings) could be "discovered" by activity-time-account-systems, which in many areas are still needed to be implemented. However, these systems are already active in many areas: as time recording systems / "stamp watches" etc. in companies and authorities. Thus, expanding these systems to other sectors – like welfare-activities and commitment-times should not be a real problem.

The systems of instructing people to work are already in place today. But can only be implemented poorly because state institutions do not have enough skills nor opportunities. Expanding global welfare and charity through well-organized systems can be a great help for all people: those who desperately need help (abroad). And also for those who need to learn again (at home) to contribute to society, which, so far, has supported them. Without them contributing to anything.

There might come aspects, like epidemics, which might force people to do nothing, to stay at home. As well in such cases, the TV-bonus system is better, than the actual capital models. People, at least will be able to continue to consume. Demand will not break down. Industry might continue to produce (at least with automized systems – and/or at lower level). No one must become unemployed. No survival-credits must be given by the state…

4.2.14   (Data) Banks

The ability to implement a new "foreign currency", means "TV" and the verifiability of accounts are key aspect and a major contribution which the existing systems from the banking sector, insurance companies, telephone companies, Internet providers etc. may provide. With their data systems the new accounts for each person can be set up, secured and verified.

Controlling is already done by many companies

and states. There is far more data about us and what we do than you can imagine. As this tendency can´t be stopped anyway, why not use these systems: for a new wealth generation on our world. The new account is nothing else, than what (money and data) banks already do and know today. Now this will be with a big bonus. With this bonus, everyone can finally do what they always have wanted to do. And at the same time contribute much more to the wealth of nations than any other system ever has done before.

A new data-bank-system should be banning any speculation. And otherwise pursue it with drastic penalties. That would be a great win. In speculation, one side wins – and all other lose. There is no general wealth growth. It leads only to a "redistribution" to the strongest.

An alternative rule, if the ban is not possible (in the first instance), would be drastic taxes on profits, as they are already being implemented in gaming casinos.

Besides many rules and prohibitions, there must exist "brakes" against too large TV losses. Since not even the top departments of top banks and financial organizations are able to speculate correctly. And even states were not able to foresee misleading tendencies. "Brake systems" are absolutely required. Success in "normal" business is difficult enough. The prosperity that TV-bonuses might achieve should not be buried in speculation.

4.2.15 Surplus generating

Any person or company working in the "productive" sector (mostly private sector, since the state should no longer be allowed to enter markets) can accumulate TV-values on their accounts, according to their "salary" or self-employment- / entrepreneur-income. Sick, unemployed or unlucky people do not fall into a deep hole. They will continue to receive the normal average TV-wage or have access to their TV-bonus-account - as they will potentially be available again to the wealth generation process.

The surplus production on the TV-account of individuals should be provided with a general deduction of X% - as a kind of tax for society. This X% should not be useable from states as before. This should be a buffer for each person for their own retirement - and for society. Society could use this surplus to reduce the number of sick or unemployment periods of its citizens. Via welfare-organizations. No state is needed for this anymore.

For surplus production on the TV-accounts of companies, there should also be general deduction of X% - as a kind of tax for society. These X% should not be used by the state to finance its own projects. This buffer should be built up for every company and for society, in order to finance bad times and realignments. If everything "goes wrong", this buffer can be used to compensate creditors. In order to not provoke additional bankruptcies.

4.2.16 Limits

All these thoughts about TV-buffer for all and many purposes, sound like a free way to use TV for all and everything.

But there is a general limit, as previously shown. The general limit is the average life-time of citizens and/or of companies. And specific limits must be set by country for private and for business. And If someone or a company "dies", his/her initial TV-bonus must be deducted - only the respective gain within lifetime will remain – and may be distributed to the remaining heirs.

Even in the universe, time is not endless - at least not endless in our definition as (matter-)"carrier-immanent". At least with respect to the things we can see or calculate at the moment. Stars also lose energy as they get older. And this can lead to an "off" as a super-nova. Or, at the crushing of a large star, even lead to a black hole.

4.2.17 (Re-)Distribution of TV-buffer

The buffer of individuals can, if they die, be transferred to i.a. their children. It can also be donated to i.a. welfare organizations. But only the additional buffer earned should be considered. The TV-bonus given at the start should be subtracted.

The same should apply to companies if they stop their activities.

When a company buys another company, it can be paid at the current value plus the additional TV-buffer as a general formula. But of course, supply and demand regulate the final price.

However, there will be far fewer takeovers than in today's world, because:

O Companies can easily get additional "money": by selling their shares to 7 billion, now wealthy, citizens of this world;
O a rule, that stocks must be held as pure hedging purchases for 10 years, can drastically reduce speculation;

O with the new wealth, there will be so much demand that all companies can go their own way. There will be no need to sell or buy.

If there are transactions, society should benefit. Through taxes on the amounts of the transactions. But politic should not be able to benefit from these taxes. Otherwise a competition of the best place to trade will start between the countries. Politic should only be responsible for the rules.
These taxes should be distributed within all welfare organizations or stored, to possibly been used in bad times.

4.2.18. Currency and values

Today there are 195 states and 160 different currencies. This is mainly due to politicians wanting to establish their own fiscal and monetary policy, to help their own economy.

The TV-introduction allows to standardize all currencies to just one: the TV, the Time-Valuta.

The value of the TV can be adjusted in any

country, in the first step, to the actual value of its currency. Within time further adjustments will result. Speculation should be banned. However, even if speculation were to be attempted, no one has enough money to influence the new dimensions with which TV is introduced. Because TV relativizes the meaning (not the value, the latter remains constant) of the money down to 1% in industrialized countries - or even to 0.1% in China - as in the previous GDP comparison shows.

Each persons TV can easily be adapted to the place where it lives. When relocating TV will be multiplied with the valid values of the corresponding area.

And since monetary policy has no money to play with, the possibilities of increasing the "money" amount, i.e. the TV, are different:

O increase birth rates - and/or
O improve health for a longer lifespan - and/or
O attract foreign investors - and/or
O advising citizens (not politically forcing) to achieve a higher education and/or
O recommend alternative training (not obstruct) in order to achieve a higher income and standard of living in the future, and/or
O reduce taxes, etc.

The point is, that the governments can no longer create additional "money" through their own "currency policy". Only improving the realistic value of their TV will help. The actual value of their assets and competitiveness will become a factor in their actual TV values.

Rising prosperity must now be achieved on a smarter way than via money-policy. Money - in the form of different currencies - should no longer be a "main tool" in an astronomy-rules-oriented economy. There is no money in the universe.

Politics must recognize and learn that the only way to increase the prosperity of its citizens is the advice that everyone must find and go his own way. The liberty of one's own way optimization - as Einstein discovered being valid for planets optimizing their orbits - should be implemented for all citizens on our earth. Politicians should not force citizens to do something what politicians think, is right.

Political interventions are forbidden on earth. There is no politics in the universe.

With TV as the instrument for transactions on a common global basis, fair trade and wealth will be achievable. More quickly than with the political

and economic unrest being caused by the continuous revaluations of 160 different currencies
within 195 countries.

And since countries no longer depend on the
loans and monetary constraints of banks and
states, they can easily break new ground and increase the prosperity of their countries. And if
there are problems with the introduction of TV,
there is enough buffer for optimizations.

4.2.19 Cash

Cash should be available for all small purchases.
But the amount of money for the mini-purchases
should be limited. This is already being done in
some countries, such as Italy. This principle could
be introduced everywhere in order to eliminate
the black market. Spain has an enormous black
market, and most of the €500 notes are in Spain.
Money and black-money must be limited as
wealth rises.

4.2.20 Inflation and Wealth

Inflation arises when too much people want to
buy scarce products or services at the same time.

With the TV-launch we will see a large increase

in demand for products and services in the first step. Inflation could be a problem at the start. This must be handled with caution. Otherwise all the new generated (potential) wealth might be destroyed.

There is no better time than today for implementing anti-inflationary systems. We have a global crisis. There is no real growth, almost nowhere. And rather than inflation, deflation is the danger.

Growth will come through all the mentioned aspects. You don't need 2% "should-be" inflation anymore. Let's "freeze" prices first. And prosecute misdeeds through the law. And for the first implementation phase, introduce a selection system for certain highly sought-after products or services: FiFo: first in, First Out. Additional demand will land on a list and gradually be processed. Actual supplier might quickly increase production and/or service levels. If they can't, people will go to (new) competition. And if the competition can't offer it, people will just have to wait - or import from other countries - or emigrate. Last but not least, the possibilities of using the own TV could be limited until everything calms down.

But prices need to be kept stable - at least in the initial waves of demand. For better controlling, TV cash should not be allowed (initially). Payments should only be possible with TV bonus cards.

All transactions in small shops that are not (yet) geared towards card payment can be made with the cash of the old currency system, which is still valid in parallel.

Prices as well could be fixed at a cost-plus-X%-basis. No inflation will be possible. And speculation will be reduced.

But the biggest impact on non-inflation will result from a symptom of the GlobalOnomy-system: wealth. All mankind is wealthy. No self-profiling with products will be present anymore. Everybody is as rich as his neighbor. The actual main focus on matter, mass-products, will be replaced by a focus on individual-products and service. And product-consumption will be replaced by wisdom-focusing – with a trend to become wise. And then, all mankind might establish at the top of the Maslow-Pyramid-of-Needs: and become transcendent. Looking for things and engagements to optimize mankind and our world. World-wide-wealth is a realistic vision.

4.2.21 Closing the Gap

The great wealth differences between countries cannot be eliminated in a short period of time. There are so many things to keep in mind that this cannot be done within a few years. But potentially this gap can be closed with TV and the application of astronomy rules. And faster than with current theories and models.

2.2.22 Time & Speed

Time and speed lead to productivity and wealth.

If we want to achieve the levels of energy- and "space"-wealth of the universe as well on our earth, we need to accelerate and increase the values of productivity in all sectors.

And since TV values will be an important part of calculations and balance sheets, in order to increase company-values, you no longer have to invest primarily in productivity-optimizing machines. It now is more important to employ more people. For the wealth of companies, countries and for the wealth of society.

"Time is money?" – OK: "Money, be time!"

G. Index

Wikipedia & Google

*¹ A Briefer History of Time (Steven Hawking with Leonard Mlodinow)

*² Astronomic Solutions, a new model of universe, (Albert Bright, 2014, British Library, ISBN 978-0-9930836-0-0)

*³ Astron-Economic Solutions, a new model of economy, (Albert Bright, 2015, British Library, ISBN 978-0-9930836-2-4)

*⁴ We defined gravity to be the "other side" of "simple-relativity"-formula of Albert Einstein, as we were able to relativize Einstein via extrapolation of Newton. Gravity as well is Energy, according to our formulas in "Astronomic Solutions" *²

*⁵ The last paragraph gets additional support from our findings (in a later published book, which will be the next to be translated: Astron-RaumOnomie, AstronSpaceOnomy*⁶):

*⁶ AstronSpaceOnomy: will be translated from the book AstronRaumOnomie (Albert Bright, 2019, tradition-Verlag, Germany)

H. Short Description

AstronTimeOnomy Solutions, is a fascinating journey into the dimensions of time.

After looking at these time dimensions, a formula for "time" is developed on the basis of the currently valid astronomy formulas. This formula relativizes time and revolutionizes insights. In the same way, Albert Bright had already relativized Einstein in his first book by extrapolating Newton; and in the 2nd book: economic challenges via astronomy rules.

When highlighting the importance of time-dimensions, Bright also relativizes the importance of money-based economy models. It shows that the misuse of "virtual money" leads to a large bubble that will explode if it is not put into perspective: with "TV", Time-Valuta, the new time-currency dimension for the economy. And since there is no equivalent to money in the universe, he comes to the conclusion:

"Time is money?" - OK: "Money, be time!"

Albert Bright shows that nowadays money can easily be replaced by TV - and suggests implementation aspects. As well aspects of how abuse can be prevented are considered. At the same time, he shows that the current focus on money and capital - will now be turned towards people, Every person on earth gets a "TV" bonus at his free disposal – and will be "rich". This is "copied" from the stars/planets, as they are "getting" a mat-ter- and energy-"bonus" (via, i.a. big-bang) for the opportunity to optimize their own orbits - as Albert Einstein discovered 100 years ago.

The universe has been growing for 13.8 billion years - and today grows even faster than ever be-fore. We can do that with our economy as well. The application of the rules and formulas of as-tronomy in economy, sociology, liberty, peace and sustainability can lead to an enormous growth of wealth: World-Wide-Wealth.

Notes:

FSC
www.fsc.org

MIX

Papier aus ver-
antwortungsvollen
Quellen

Paper from
responsible sources

FSC® C105338

.